Copyright © 2021 Tracy Forrester
All rights reserved.

ISBN: 9798512039977
Imprint: Independently published

Contents

Introduction 9

Chapter 1 Introduction to the Problem-Solving Process 13

    A Structured Approach 14

    The 8 Step Problem-Solving Approach Description 16

    Problem-Solving Tools Selection Guide 18

    Case Study: Forrester Agricultural Products, Inc. 20

Chapter 2 21

Step 1: Validating the Problem and Selecting the Correct Approach 21

    The Primary Purposes for Step 1 22

    Emergency Action Plan 24

    Work to Satisfy the Customer 25

    Quality Alert 25

    Containment Worksheet 28

    Containment Check Sheet 29

    8 Step Problem Solving Method Application Guidelines 32

    Special Cause Variation Examples 35

    Some Issues that may warrant a formal 8 Step Problem Solving approach 36

    Some Issues that may Require a Different Methodology 36

    Applying the Problem-Solving methods application criteria to the Forrester Agricultural Products, Inc. case study 37

    Benchmarking 38

    Emergency Action Plan 39

    Step 1: Pointers and Pitfalls 39

    Documenting Step 1 within the 8 Step format 41

Chapter 3 43

Step 2: Team Member Selection and Recruitment 43

    RASIC Matrix 44

    Step 2 Pointers and Pitfalls 46

    Documenting Step 2 within the 8 Step format 48

Chapter 4 49
Step 3: Problem Statement 49

    5W2H Matrix 52

    5W2H Matrix for Forrester Agricultural Products, Inc. Case Study 53

    Problem Statement Example 1 53

    Problem Statement Example 2 53

    Problem Statement Example 3 54

    Step 3 Pointers and Pitfalls 55

    Documenting Step 3 within the 8 Step format 56

Chapter 5 57
Step 4: Containment & Interim Corrective 57
Actions 57

    Steps to Identify and Implement Temporary Corrective Actions 59

    Action Plan 60

    Step 4 Pointers and Pitfalls 61

    Documenting Step 4 within the 8 Step format 62

Chapter 6 63
Step 5: Root Cause Analysis 63

    Is it a Symptom, or a Root Cause? 64

    The Root Cause, or a Source? 64

    The Owl Approach to Problem Solving 65

    Focus on the Process when Looking for the Root Cause 65

    The Root Cause Analysis must be Intentional and Focused 67

    Root Cause Categories 68

        Specific Root Cause: 69

        Detection Root Cause: 69

        Systemic Root Cause: 69

    Understanding Change Points 70

        Types of Change Points 70

        Identifying the Change Point 70

    Identifying the Root Cause(s) 71

List of Common Steps for Conducting a Root Cause Analysis 71
Detailed Common Steps for Conducting a Root Cause Analysis 72
    1. Review the Problem Statement 72
    2. Review relevant data and information 72
    3. Go to the Process! 73
    4. Interview process experts 74
    5. Brainstorming 74
    6. Fishbone Diagram (Cause and Effect Diagram) 76
        Which Potential Cause to Pursue? 81
        Nominal Group Technique 81
        The Source of the Problem 83
    7. 5-Why Analysis 84
        3 Legged 5 Why Analysis 85
        Steps for completing the 5 Whys Analysis 87
        Review of FAPI Why Made 5 Why Analysis 90
        Make sure the Root Cause is about the Process 90
        Test for linearity 91
    8. Return to the Process and Verify Root Cause(s) 93
Root Cause for Why Not Detected 95
What is "Why Not Detected"? 95
Why did the Inspection Process Fail? 95
Why Not Detected? (Examples) 95
5 Why Analysis for Why Not Detected 96
Step 5 Pointers and Pitfalls 99
Documenting Step 5 within the 8 Step format 100

Chapter 7 101
Step 6: Permanent Corrective Action 101
Selection, Implementation, and Validation 101
Corrective Action Selection 102
Simple Corrective Action Selection Method – PICK Chart 103
PICK Chart Instructions 104

    Validation 106

    Step 6 Pointers and Pitfalls 108

    Documenting Step 6 within the 8 Step format 109

Chapter 8 .... **111**

Step 7: Preventive Actions Implementation and Verification **111**

    Preventive Actions 111

    Steps to Determining Preventive Actions 113

    Update the Control Plan 113

    Update the FMEA 115

    Feed Across/Feed Forward 116

    Step 7: Pointers and Pitfalls 119

    Documenting Step 7 within the 8 Step format 120

Chapter 9 .... **121**

Step 8: Celebrate Team Success! **121**

    Step 8: Pointers and Pitfalls 123

    Documenting Step 8 within the 8 Step format 124

Chapter 10 .... **125**

Establishing a Culture for Problem Solving **125**

    Accountability 126

    Learning and Reinforcing the Language of Problem Solving 127

    Typical Problem-Solving Languages 129

Chapter 11 .... **131**

Problem-Solving Process Management **131**

    Problem Solving Review Team 131

    8-Step Evaluation Check List 132

    Problem Solving Review Team Process Map 134

Selected Problem-Solving Tools **135**

    5W/2H Tool (Used in Step 3) 136

    Action Plan (Used in Steps 1, 4, 6, & 7) 138

    Benchmarking (Used in steps 5, 6, & 7) 139

    Brainstorming (Used in Step 5) 140

Capability Study & Analysis (Used in Step 7) 142

Cause & Effect Diagram (Used in Step 5) 144

Check Sheet (Used in Steps 1, 4, and 7) 145

Containment Worksheet (Used in Steps 1 and 4) 146

Error Proofing/Mistake Proofing Used in steps 6 & 7) 148

Feed Across/Feed Forward (Used in Steps 1 & 7) 150

FMEA (Used in steps 5, 6, & 7) 151

Gage R & R Study (Used in Steps 5 & 6) 153

Gemba Walk (Used in any/all steps) 155

Layered Process Audit (Used in steps 7 & 8) 156

Lessons Learned (Used in steps 5, 6, 7 & 8) 159

Measles Chart (Used in Steps 5 & 7) 160

Pareto Diagram (Used in Steps 3, 5 & 7) 164

PICK Chart (Used in Steps 6 & 7) 165

Process Flow Chart (Used in all Steps) 166

RASIC Matrix (Used in Step 2) 168

Trend Chart (Used in Steps 1, 3, 5, 6, & 7) 169

Bibliography 173

Introduction

Problem Solving, or Problem Fixing? The two terms may seem similar and are even used synonymously by some, but to a trained and experienced Quality or CI Practitioner, the two terms carry with them very different implications. Problem Solving is often structured, methodical, and permanent while Problem Fixing is often more immediate, more focused on adjusting the process, often temporary, and due to the general lack of thoroughness, is admittedly quicker. The table in Figure I.1 highlights some of the differences between Problem Solving and Problem Fixing.

Typical Characteristics of Problem Solving vs Problem Fixing	
Problem Solving	Problem Fixing
Identifies Root Cause of Problem	Identifies Source of Problem
Result is Permanent	Result is Temporary
Focus on Corrective Action	Focus on Process Correction
Long-term Thinking	Short-term Thinking
Preventive Measures	Fire Fighting
Feed Forward/Feed Across	Localized Actions

Figure I.1 Problem Solving vs Problem Fixing

Even though the table shows that there are stark differences between the two approaches, it is not as easy as just choosing Problem Solving over Problem Fixing as the approach to take because it is not always left to the individual to determine which course of action to pursue. In a business setting, much of what drives a person down one path or the other is often cultural to the business and by the very nature of culture, extends far beyond the willingness of someone to embrace one methodology over another.

Historical Approaches to Problem Solving

Throughout the course of history, there have been many different approaches and methods employed to solve problems. These methods have varied in degrees of sophistication throughout time, but many of the tools and methods that are frequently used today got their origins decades or longer ago.

The 5W2H has its origins in the first century AD. The 5 Why Anlaysis from Toyota in Japan dates to the 1930s. The Plan Do Study Act, (PDSA), cycle got its origins from Walter Shewhart in the 1930s with a simple 3 step model that was later enhanced by Dr. Deming. In the 1940s Toyota introduced the A3 method. In the 1980s the US Government, (via the Military), presented a 7 step method for structured Problem Solving. Also in the 1980s, Ford rolled out their 8D method and Motorola introduced a formal Six Sigma approach.

Over the course of the past 50 years, structured Problem Solving has been embraced by countless organizations as a necessary element of improving Safety, Quality, and other business results by permanently solving problems and by preventing the same problems from recurring. The nature of these organizations range in scope from nonprofit, to Educational, Aerospace, Automotive, Communications, and even the Military.

The primary aim of this book is to present an approach for Problem Solving and to help equip someone with a proven structure, tools, and nuanced explanation necessary to be successful at Problem Solving. Throughout this book, I will present an approach, (and some useful tools), to Problem Solving that has proven effective at solving problems and preventing their recurrence in several global industries and organizations.

Chapter 1

Introduction to the Problem-Solving Process

Before going very far down the path of explaining a Problem-Solving process, it would be a mistake to assume that everyone knows what the term "Problem-Solving Process" means and instead we will commit a little time working to define it.

If we break down the term "Problem-Solving Process", a couple of things will become clear. The word "Process" implies that there is a structured approach. Merriam-Webster dictionary defines process as "A series of actions or operations conducing to an end", (Merriam-Webster, 2021). The word "series" in the definition indicates successive actions. So, the use of the word *process* implies that there is a structured approach with linear steps.

The American Society for Quality, (ASQ), provides the following definition of the term Problem Solving: "Problem solving is the act of defining a problem; determining the cause of the problem; identifying, prioritizing, and selecting alternatives for a solution; and implementing a solution", (ASQ, 2021).

Based on these definitions, we should be able to draw some simple conclusions regarding what "Problem-Solving Process" means:
1. The term "Problem-Solving Process" implies that a process is used to solve problems.
2. This further implies that the process is linear.
3. The process is structured.
4. The Problem-Solving process requires specific and defined steps.
5. The term "Problem Solving" implies that once "solved", the problem does not continue to recur.
6. It is further implied that we are not just correcting the immediate process failure, but that the correction is permanent and sustainable, (or else it will recur).

Based on the breakdown of the term, we can develop a working definition of the "Problem-Solving Process" to be: "A structured approach to Problem Solving utilizing a linear series of steps to identify a problem's root cause and implementing permanent corrective and preventive actions to prevent recurrence".

A Structured Approach
The approach we focus on in this book is the 8 Step Problem-Solving approach that somewhat follows the Ford 8D format. The reason for selecting the 8 Step method is because it works and because the individual steps and tools employed in the 8 Step method can be used to follow most of the other structured Problem-Solving approaches mentioned earlier. In other

words, most other approaches use tools and methods that are comprised of what is included in the 8 Step approach.

Another thing we will focus on in this Problem-Solving guide is the process that yielded the failure. While it may be easy to get caught up in focusing Problem-Solving efforts on the problem itself, as we will soon see, *fixing* a problem will only improve the current condition and the current instance of a failure. This typically does little to nothing to address real root causes and preventing their future recurrence. When we focus on the problem and not the process, we run the risk of failing to completely analyze the process for the root cause and corrective actions. As is the case with trying harder and re-training the operator, focusing on just the problem instead of the process will not yield the expected results.

The 8 Step Problem-Solving methodology is intended to be a linear process with the success of each step dependent on the quality and thoroughness of the work that was done in the previous step. The process is also intended to be conducted utilizing a cross-functional team approach. The process will not yield optimum results in the absence of either of these approaches.

This book will detail each step of the process and the tools utilized in that step, to solve a problem detailed in a case study scenario from a fictitious manufacturing company named Forrester Agricultural Products, Inc. Each chapter will include various pointers and pitfalls to watch out for in that step, an identification of the tools that can be helpful in that step and a completion of the documentation of the Problem-Solving work from that step.

The 8 Step Problem-Solving Approach Description

1. Step 1: Validating the Problem and Selecting the Correct Approach
    - Step 1 includes performing enough analysis to determine whether the 8 Step Problem Solving approach is the correct approach to solve the given problem.
2. Step 2: Team Member Selection and Recruitment
    - Step 2 walks through a formal approach to ensuring the right number of the right people are recruited and selected as team members for the Problem-Solving process
3. Step 3: Problem Statement
    - Step 3 is a detailed approach for clearly defining and describing the problem in terms that provide direction and parameters for the rest of the Problem-Solving steps.
4. Step 4: Containment & Temporary Corrective Actions
    - Step 4 ensures that short-term actions are implemented to contain the problem, (and protect the customer), until permanent actions are later implemented.
5. Step 5: Root Cause Analysis
    - Step 5 provides formal tools and steps to take for determining the root cause(s) of the problem.
6. Step 6: Permanent Corrective Action Identification, Selection, Implementation, Verification and Validation
    - Step 6 ensures that the proper actions are implemented to correct the process and to prevent the root cause from recurring.
7. Step 7: Preventive Actions and Validation
    - Step 7 follows steps to ensure the necessary actions are taken to institutionalize the corrective actions and to prevent future recurrence in other application areas.

8. Step 8: Celebrate Team Success
    - ➤ Step 8 in critical to the Problem-Solving culture by ensuring members of successful Problem-Solving teams are properly recognized.

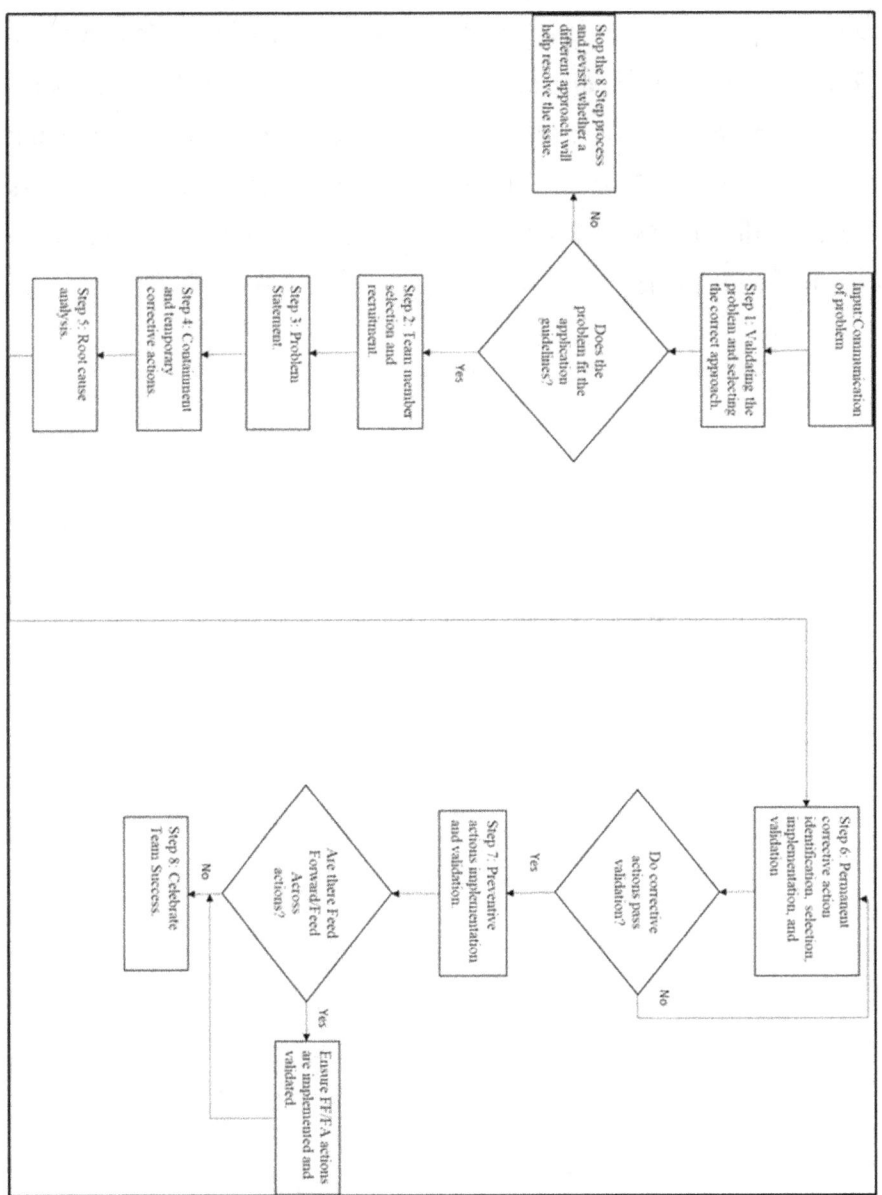

Figure 1.1 8-Step Problem-Solving Process

Problem-Solving Tools Selection Guide

The Problem-Solving Tools Selection Guide is intended to provide a guideline for selecting the appropriate Problem-Solving tools for each step in the 8 Step Problem-Solving process. Many of these tools are described within the applicable step throughout the book and many are also addressed with descriptions and examples in the "Selected Problem-Solving Tools" section near the back of this book. These are not the only Problem-Solving tools that are available for experienced and knowledgeable Problem Solvers to use, but they are generally basic enough for a novice to use with little instruction and practice.

Problem Solving Tool	0	1	2	3	4	5	6	7	8
5W/2H Tool			X						
5-Why Analysis					X				
8 Step Report		X	X	X	X	X	X	X	X
Affinity Diagram					X				
Application Guidelines	X								
Benchmarking	X	X	X	X	X	X	X	X	
Brainstorming					X				
Capability Study					X		X		
Check Sheet			X			X	X		
Control Plan				X	X	X		X	
Error Proofing						X	X		
Feed Forward/Feed Across								X	
Fishbone Diagram					X				
FMEA				X	X	X		X	
Gage R&R Study					X		X		
Gemba (Go and See)			X	X	X	X	X	X	
Is/is-Not Tool			X						
KPI/Metrics Chart			X			X	X		
Layered process Audits							X	X	
Lessons Learned					X	X		X	
Measles Chart			X		X	X	X		
Multi-Voting					X				
Nominal Group Technique (NGT)					X				
Nonconforrmance notification		X	X						
Pareto Chart			X		X	X	X		
Paynter Chart			X			X	X		
Plan, Do, Check, Act				X	X	X	X		
Process Flow Chart			X	X	X			X	
Quality Alert/Heads Up				X					
Tool Selection Guidelines	X								
Trend Chart			X		X	X	X		
Value Stream Mapping			X						

Figure 1.2 Problem-Solving Tools Selection Guide

Case Study: Forrester Agricultural Products, Inc.

Forrester Agricultural Products, Inc., (FAPI), is a manufacturing company that produces a variety of feed systems for growers of livestock and poultry. Being somewhat vertically integrated, FAPI manufacturers some of the components needed for the systems and they also complete the assembly and finishing work.

One of the key components that goes into the poultry feeders is a drive system which contains a gear box that is powered by a motor and in turn, powers the auger system. The gears that go into the gear box are also made in a mfg. plant owned by FAPI.

On May 12, 2018, at 3:47 PM, FAPI Assy. Quality Manager called the mfg. plant Quality Manager and informed her that they had received a concern from a customer stating that since they switched to a new FAPI feeder system, the chickens are not eating enough. The FAPI Assy. QM reported that a group of Engineers worked with the customer and found that the system had an audible ticking noise and slight vibration and they determined that it appeared to be within the gearbox and not the auger or another part of the system.

Utilizing the available traceability information from the feeder system serial number, an initial investigation at FAPI revealed that the gear box was produced on February 5, 2018. The gear box was returned to FAPI Mfg. for inspection and evaluation. The noise level from the gearbox was found to be out of spec. Upon disassembly of the gearbox, it was noted that the gear lube looked clean and at the correct fill level. There was no visible debris or contamination present. The gears were removed and inspected in the lab for tooth profile, backlash, lead error, indexing error, Pitch Diameter, PD runout, and ID-PD runout.

All characteristics measured during the returns analysis were found to measure in spec. The gears were further inspected against a master gear and small raised surfaces from indentations were found on some gear teeth. The raised surfaces were removed, and the gearbox was reassembled. The noise level was measured and found to be within spec at this point. At this point, the immediate problem has been fixed, but the underlying root causes have not been permanently solved.

Figure 1.3 Forrester Agricultural Products, Inc – Case Study

Chapter 2

Step 1: Validating the Problem and Selecting the Correct Approach

Step 1 is a crucial step in the Problem-Solving process as it sets the tone for the subsequent steps in the Problem-Solving process. In step 1 we will determine whether a nonconformance even exists. This may sound obvious to some, but confirming, or agreeing, that there is a nonconformance is critical for many reasons, not the least of which is to protect your organization from accepting related costs and liability when it is not warranted. As we will discuss in other sections throughout the book, the reporter of a problem is often reporting on symptoms and they normally will not have insight into causes of the problem, and in some cases, even the source. Given this, it is crucial that the party receiving notification of a nonconformance takes the necessary steps to confirm agreement of the nonconformance.

To expand a little on the message from the previous paragraph, proving that a nonconformance does not exist as presented does not grant license to ignore the idea that while the nonconformance was not valid as presented, it is still possible that a very real problem does exist. The customer, or consumer of the product, transaction, or service, is having some kind of issue and a great approach here may be to work with them to determine what the real issue is and to try to help them troubleshoot it to ensure the responsibility is aimed in the correct direction. Doing this will not only help your organization avoid unnecessary responsibility, but it may also help to build and strengthen relationships with that entity.

Another important part of step 1 includes taking the necessary steps to ensure that relevant emergency actions are taken. The need for emergency actions is based on the perceived and evaluated risk to your customer and to your organization. In short, emergency actions are more necessary in some situations than in other situations and the need for and depth of emergency actions should be evaluated and agreed to.

The Primary Purposes for Step 1
1. Provide Emergency Response Actions, (ERA), if necessary.
2. Evaluate the need and applicability for following this structured Problem-Solving process by using the Problem-Solving Application Criteria to determine whether the process is suitable for the issue of concern.
3. Collect relevant, initial information from the reporting source and from the originating process to enable use by the Problem-Solving team going forward, if necessary.

Prior to opening a formal Problem-Solving process, the necessary level of leadership should determine that it is an appropriate method to employ for solving the problem. Chapter 2 will walk through how to follow the Problem-Solving process through Step 1. Step 1 is also the only step in the 8 Step process that does not utilize a full and formal Problem-Solving team to complete. This is primarily due to the need to react with immediate urgency to ensure the affected party recovers from the problem quickly and with as little negative impact as possible.

1. Because the formal Problem-Solving team will not be recruited and assembled until step 2, the owner, or assignee of the issue must do some of the work in step 1 with an ad hoc team that is comprised of personnel who are typically engaged at the initial onset of the type of issue that is being addressed. An example of this may be a Quality Engineer engaging a Process Engineer, or Production Manager for a quality-related issue. In the case of a quality issue with product, the Quality Engineer will typically take the following initial steps:

2. Quickly communicate with the reporter of the issue to gather all available relevant information, (as applicable), including what the symptom of the issue is, the current impact on and status of the reporter's process, the quantity of product involved, current inventory levels, any required Emergency Actions from the customer's perspective, and any available traceability information from the suspect product.

3. Issue communications to relevant internal parties, (a Quality Alert is one example).

4. Gather an ad hoc team to work through the necessary Emergency Actions.

5. Work to determine inventory levels, containment, and to mobilize people to act as needed.

Emergency Action Plan

Emergency Action Plans, (EAPs), are sometimes required as an initial, immediate response to a problem. The best way to determine if and to what extent an EAP is required is to communicate with the customer, or reporter of the problem. Sometimes the customer will require some specific EAPs. When there is not a clearly expressed requirement for an EAP, it is up to the initial owner of the problem to determine the need level. This may be done with counsel from a committee, supervisor, or co-worker, but it must be done quickly.

A *typical* initial response to a Quality problem at a customer location involving defective product often follows some or all of the steps below:

1. Immediately communicate with the customer.
2. Immediately communicate with necessary personnel internally.
3. Determine if product is in route or is going to be shipped soon and stop shipments. The same approach applies to stopping a service.
4. Determine with the customer whether immediate containment is required at their location, or if they want their inventory replaced with certified product.
5. Quarantine all inventory at all locations.
6. Develop a containment method.
7. Prepare, train, and distribute a Quality Alert.
8. Prepare a Containment Worksheet to ensure all inventory is accounted for.
9. Initiate containment.
10. Report on containment results.

Notes: Urgency and communication are keys to the success of any EAP. The goal is to limit disruption to your customer, (external or internal), and thereby also reducing risk to your own organization. When this step is not done thoroughly, the impact of related customer dissatisfaction can be immeasurable. The last thing needed once a problem is identified and reported by a customer is a slow, or inadequate response.

Work to Satisfy the Customer

In the FAPI case study, the customer is concerned and the issue with the feeder is adversely affecting their operation and overall business. Because the root cause of the noise issue is unknown at this time, FAPI agreed to send a replacement gearbox to install on the feeder system. This is not always as straight forward as it sounds because given the unknown root cause of the issue, the replacement gearbox could have the same issue which would be adding insult to injury. (I have often told my own Quality teams that one issue may be forgiven if effectively managed, but a repeat issue is much less likely to be forgiven).

In this case, some of the initial analysis of the returned gear box included measuring the noise level. This noise measurement was then compared to other gear boxes and a gear box with a noise level measuring on the lower end of those measured was used as the replacement for the customer. Once installed, the replacement gear box worked as intended and this specific occurrence of the problem was corrected. These actions should be noted on the EAP Action Plan. (Note: It is necessary to point out here that while the symptom from the specific incident was resolved with the replacement of the gear box, the root cause is still unknown and the problem itself remains unsolved).

Quality Alert

A Quality Alert is a simple communication tool. The Quality Alert is typically a one-page summary of an issue that when done well, shows as much as it says. It should be visual to quickly show someone what is wrong with what. The Quality Alert format should be controlled and consistent from one to the next. They should be serialized and controlled within a single function. There should be a defined distribution. The Quality Alert will become part of the Problem-Solving record, so make sure it is useful, clear, and accurate.

The primary purpose for the Quality Alert is to communicate important information regarding a problem and any immediate containment steps. The format may vary from company to company as there is not any single way to do this. The important thing to remember is that there should be some process and mechanism in place to communicate issues with sufficient details to adequately communicate what the problem is, who it has affected, visual examples if possible, and any required containment actions.

It is crucial that all affected employees are trained and sign-off on training of the Quality Alert. When the value of the Quality Alert is not understood by the creator/issuer, it is common for someone to simply prepare the Quality Alert and send it in emails or post it on a board in the relevant areas of the organization. If the intended purpose for the Quality Alert is to ensure that all affected personnel are fully aware of the issue, the perceived risk, and required actions then it is necessary to personally communicate the information and to own the communication. This cannot be accomplished by posting it on a board or by putting it on someone's desk while they are at lunch.

Quality Alert – from Forrester Agricultural Products, Inc. Case Study

FAPI Quality Alert!

Customer Name:	Irish Poultry Products, Inc.	Quality Alert #:	20-012
Product/WO:	N/A	Date Effective:	5/12/2018
Issued By:	T. Forrester	Expiration Date:	6/12/2018
Dept(s):	Production, Quality, Shipping, Engineering		

Issue Description (Picture/Sketch)

FAPI Assy Dept. received a complaint from their external customer and investigations determined that there are dents/dings on some gear teeth in the gearbox.

Chart for Gear Teeth Defects

- Category 1 • 1mm
- Category 2 o 1.5mm
- Category 3 O 2mm
- Category 4 O 2.5mm

ACCEPTED
CUSTOMER: Forrester Ag Products, Inc.
WO. NO. ___ DATE 5/12/2018
NO. PCS: 72
PART NO. 123-XYZ   MATERIAL ___ SER. NO. ___
PART NAME: Spur Gear
INSPECTOR: Natalie Forrester
COMMENTS: 100% Inspected for Dents

Dent

Required Action(s):

1) Move product, 1 box at a time from the quarantine area to the containment area.
2) At the beginning of each shift and upon returning from breaks, compare the tagged samples to the Mylar Chart for Gear Teeth Defects and ensure you agree with the labeled sizes of the defects.
3) Remove gears from the box and visually inspect all gear teeth for dents/damage. Inspect in well-lit area.
4) If a gear tooth defect is found, compare it to the Mylar Chart for Gear Teeth Defects and ensure that the defect is not larger than the size of the circle on Category 2.
5) Once all gears in the box have been measured, identify on green "Accepted" label "100% Inspected for Dents"
6) If any other defect is found during inspection, contact QC Dept immediately
7) Turn in completed check sheet at the end of the shift

Sign-Offs: (If more signature space needed, sign on back of Quality Alert)

Print Name:	Sign Name:
Alyssa B.	*Alyssa Brown*
Alex F.	*Alex Forrester*
Thomas W.	*Thomas Wenzlick*
Dalton G.	*Dalton Grubb*
Logan F.	*Logan Forrester*
Hannah F.	*Hannah Forrester*

Figure 2.1 FAPI Quality Alert

Containment Worksheet

The containment worksheet is a tool that is useful to help account for every unit of inventory in the value stream when the severity and risk of a unit not being accounted for during containment is relatively high. (Each organization must determine what high severity and high risk means to them as these are relative terms that vary by industry, organization, and by product, or service function.)

One of the primary reasons for a defective unit or service being received by a customer after an issue has been communicated is failed containment. One reason containments fail is because proper measures were not taken to ensure that every unit in the pipeline was properly accounted for.

The containment worksheet works by the user defining every possible inventory location throughout the process and then determining the quantity of inventory expected at each location. The expected inventory quantity is the inventory quantity listed in the ERP system, or other inventory system. Once the containment worksheet is populated with the expected inventory numbers for each location, a physical count and quarantine is done to ensure the physical number matches the expected number from the ERP system. If there is a difference between the quantity listed in the inventory system and the physical count, the numbers must be reconciled. This is a critical step because if one unit is unaccounted for at this point it can cause the problem to recur at the customer. Once the inventory quantities are reconciled and all inventory is quarantined, the physical inspection can be started.

Forrester Agricultural Products, Inc. Containment Worksheet

Date: 12-May-18

Issue Lead: Natalie Forrester

Part Number(s): 123-XYZ

Issue Description: Dents/Dings found on Gear Teeth

Location / Area	ERP Qty	Actual Qty	Qty Pass	Qty Fail	Required Action	Date
Shipping Area	288	288	288	0		5/12/2018
Receiving Area	0	0	0	0		5/12/2018
In Transit from Supplier	0	0	0	0		5/12/2018
Component Cell(s)	326	326	326	0		5/12/2018
Assembly Cell(s)/Line(s)	0	0	0	0		5/12/2018
Hold Area	0	0	0	0		5/12/2018
Warehouse	1728	1728	1728	0		5/12/2018
Staged for truck	0	0	0	0		5/12/2018
In Transit to Customer	0	0	0	0		5/12/2018
At Customer	1728	1728	1727	1	1. Issued RMA to customer and will contain product once received at FAPI. 2. Tag rejected part and send to QA lab for further analysis	5/14/2018
At Outside Processor	0	0	0	0		5/12/2018
Samples in QA Lab	6	6	6	0		5/12/2018
1st Article Board at Machine Cells	4	4	4	0		5/12/2018
Other Loc.						
Other Loc.						
Total Inventory Qty:	4080	4080				

Note: The SAP Qty and the Actual Qty MUST match! If there is a variance, follow the reaction plan below.

Reaction Plan for Inventory Discrepancy: Contact both the QA Mgr and the Materials Planning Mgr immediately to determine next course of action.

Figure 2.2 Containment Worksheet

Containment Check Sheet

We previously discussed and demonstrated the use and importance of the containment worksheet. Now, we are ready to inspect the product identified on the containment worksheet per the instructions on the Quality Alert, or other containment work instructions. We will complete the inspection part of the containment and will use a check sheet to record and report the results of the containment.

Check sheets have long been considered one of the 7 Basic Quality Tools. A check sheet is simply a structured, prepared form used for collecting data for further analysis and reporting. In this case, a check sheet was prepared to collect data from the containment inspections being performed on the contained product for the Forrester Agricultural Products, Inc. case.

In reviewing the check sheet one can see that it contains a lot of information including lot traceability information, the quantity in each container or lot, the number of any defective units identified within a specific lot, who inspected the product, and what actions were taken regarding any defective product. The information collected on the check sheet will be used by the Problem-Solving team later to understand more about the size of the problem and when and at what frequency the problem may be occurring.

Forrester Agricultural Products, Inc. Containment Checksheet

Date:	12-May-18			Issue Leader:	Natalie Forrester	
Part Number(s):	123-XYZ					
Issue Description:	Gear Teeth found with Dents/Dings					

Box/Lot Number	Box Qty	Excessive Dings/Den	Defects Other	Defects Other	Responsible for Verification	Actions taken	Date
Example (Lot 042218-1)	72	1	0	0	Scott B.	Stoned flat the Dents/Dings	5/12/2018
Lot 042218-1	72	16	1	0	Audra F.	Replaced part with known good part	5/12/2018
Lot 042218-2	72	9	0	0	Colin B.	Stoned flat the Dents/Dings	5/12/2018
Lot 042218-3	72	12	0	0	Braxston F.	Stoned flat the Dents/Dings	5/12/2018
Lot 042218-4	72	14	0	0	Delani L.		5/12/2018
Lot 042218-5	72	9	0	0	Kairi W.	Stoned flat the Dents/Dings	5/12/2018
Lot 042218-6	60	3	0	0	Weston W.	Stoned flat the Dents/Dings	5/12/2018
Lot 042218-7	72	0	0	0	Callum F.	Stoned flat the Dents/Dings	5/12/2018
Lot 042218-8	72	2	0	0	Malcolm F.	Stoned flat the Dents/Dings	5/12/2018
Totals per Shift	564	65	1	0			

Turn in checksheet to QC office at the end of each shift
Reaction Plan for Defects Identified: Contact QA Mgr immediately if "other" defects found (other than primary containment reason).

Figure 2.3 Containment Check sheet

8 Step Problem Solving Method Application Guidelines

The 8 Step Problem Solving Application Guidelines are included as a simple series of items to check off as a means of ensuring the 8 Step process is the correct approach for a given problem. The value of having many different Problem-Solving tools and approaches at our disposal lies in the assurance that we can identify the root cause of an issue and prevent its recurrence when we properly apply the correct approach. This set of guidelines helps us to assure that we are using the correct approach for the given problem.

> At a minimum, determine the following prior to applying this Problem-Solving process:
> 1. Analysis of data used to define the symptom(s) demonstrate that a nonconformance, or verified problem exists.
> 2. The problem is serious enough to allocate the resources necessary to permanently solve and correct the problem.
> 3. The problem appears to exceed the complexity, or workload for one person to readily resolve ("readily resolve" = 1 hour)
> 4. The problem is related to, (or can be reduced to), a specific occurrence.
> 5. Available data indicates that the problem was due to an incidence of special cause variation.

Figure 2.4 Application Guidelines

1. Analysis of data used to define the symptom(s) demonstrates that a nonconformance, or verified problem exists.

Confirm that a nonconformance exists. The test in this step requires a simple understanding of the difference between Problem Solving and continuous improvement. If there is not a violation of a specification or other requirement, then it is likely not a great candidate for this approach. Having said that, there may still be real interest in improving a product or process though a different approach, like continuous improvement. Confirming that a nonconformance does not exist is not a license to tell your customer that you cannot help them. In fact, it may be a great opportunity to let them know that even though there is not a nonconformance, you would love to work with them to help improve the situation for them.

2. The problem is serious enough to allocate the resources necessary to permanently solve and correct the problem.

What does this mean? This statement is important to consider because most organizations do not have the resources to apply this structured approach to solving every issue that comes up. To ensure resources are applied to those issues that have the biggest impact, or assumed risk, we must apply some level of vetting of the issues. Doing this requires that some review be completed, and that some decision be made regarding the seriousness of the issue.

Organizations evaluate the seriousness of issues for escalation through a variety of methods. Some organizations base the decision on risk, (either known or perceived), as it relates to safety, the customer, regulatory, or financial impact. Some organizations use risk to safety, regulatory, and financial impact as the minimum starting points to clear for basing the escalation decisions on something else entirely like the total number of units involved, or categories of customers. The point is that when the organization is limited in its ability to react to every issue with a structured, disciplined Problem-Solving approach, the organization needs to develop a method to ensure that the resources required to follow a structured approach to problem solving are applied to the higher risk issues.

When evaluating risk relative to Problem Solving, consider the following simple guidelines for when to apply this formal, structured Problem-Solving process:

1. Does the problem include a real, or potential human injury?
2. Does the problem involve a failure to meet regulatory requirements?
3. May the problem negatively impact the environment?
4. Was the problem reported by a customer?

5. Does the problem lead to a failure to meet KPIs that are linked to strategic objectives?

While this may not be an exhaustive list of considerations, a leader should consider these items as minimum indicators that a problem is serious enough to employ this Problem-Solving approach.

3. The problem appears to exceed the complexity, or workload for one person to readily remedy.

Determining problem complexity can be a difficult thing to consistently analyze and it becomes more difficult without some simple guidelines to assist the leader. While there are many things to consider when assigning levels of complexity, a few more obvious considerations are listed below:

1. Is the problem related to a product that is part of a complex assembly consisting of numerous components?
2. Is the problem related to a product that has very precise tolerances?
3. Is the problem related to a process that includes numerous steps and multiple process streams?
4. Are the materials involved hyper-sensitive to environmental conditions?
5. Has the problem recurred after being "solved" in the past?
6. Is the problem likely to take more than one person, or more than one hour to solve?

If the answers to any of these questions is yes, the leader should strongly consider forming a team and employing the structured Problem-Solving approach outlined in this book.

4. The problem is related to, (or can be reduced to), a specific occurrence.

This step is as much for narrowing the scope of the problem as it is a real test. If a problem includes numerous occurrences within a specific category, narrow the focus of the Problem-Solving initiative to a single, recent occurrence. The point is to not get distracted by trying to investigate and solve numerous issues at the same time. Once a single occurrence of the problem has truly been solved, the corrective and preventive actions can be applied to the process to eliminate future occurrence and the solution(s) may be applied to other and future processes through Feed Forward/Feed Across process which we will discuss in detail later.

5. Available data indicates that the problem was due to an occurrence of special cause variation.

Available data indicates that the problem was due to an occurrence of special cause variation.

Special Cause Variation is exhibited by a change in the process. This change point may be presented as a sudden shift, an ongoing trend, or a sudden change yielding an out of tolerance, (or out of control), result.

Common Cause Variation is exhibited by random variation in a process that cannot be attributed to some sudden change. Common cause variation is inherent of the capability of the process.

This 8 Step structured Problem-Solving process is more useful for solving problems related to special causes of process variation where the cause is resulting from a specific change point.

Special Cause Variation Examples

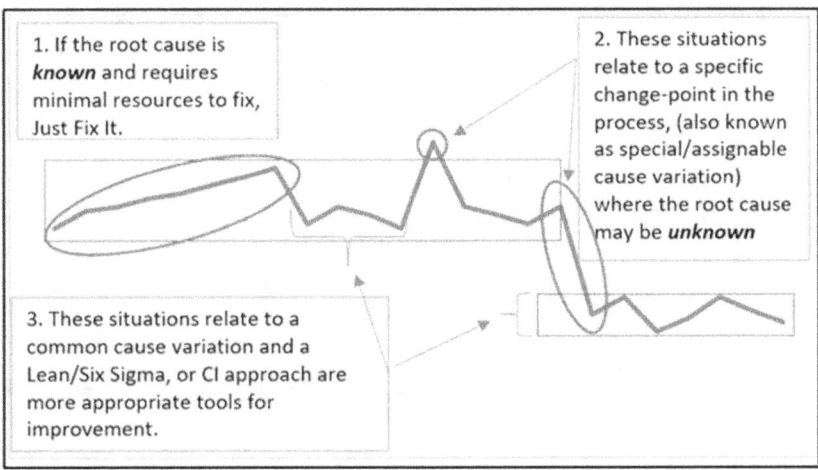

Figure 2.5 Special Cause Variation Examples

It *is* recommended that the 8 Step Problem Solving process be applied to specific failures related to specific incidents and change points, (i.e., a specific customer concern or internal incident).

It *is not* recommended to apply the 8 Step process to expansive issues related to multiple problems, products, processes, etc., (i.e., a dimensional, visual, or clerical issue on all transactions, products, or services).

Note: This Problem-Solving methodology can still be applied to solving this type of problem, but only after a specific representative incident has been selected to apply this Problem-Solving process to. Once the specific occurrence of the problem has been solved, the team will feed across the corrective and preventive actions to the other areas as applicable.

Some Issues that may Warrant a Formal 8 Step Problem Solving approach

1. Required by a customer for delivery of nonconforming product, or service.
2. A proportionally high number of customer concerns within a category.
3. To improve a metric that is operating in an out of tolerance condition.
4. In reaction to a safety incident.
5. To correct a shop floor quality issue.
6. To correct deficiencies identified on an audit.

Some Issues that may Require a Different Improvement Methodology

1. A problem where the cause is known, and the required resources are minimal – A "Just Do It" project may be the appropriate approach (Be cautious to ensure that RCA techniques were used to determine root cause)
2. An issue where there *is not* an out-of-tolerance condition and current improvement strategy is yielding some improvement,

Continuous Improvement, (incremental improvement), may be the appropriate strategy.

3. A problem that is likely to require a major process redesign, or major facility layout modifications - A Kaizen event using some of the Problem-Solving tools may be a more appropriate tool here.

4. A problem that is likely to require the analysis of multiple process variables and their individual and collective effects on the problem - A Six Sigma project may be a more appropriate tool for this application.

5. The key in getting started is to make sure you are using the correct tool for the job. Remember, **"To a man with only a hammer, everything looks like a nail"**.

Applying the Problem-Solving methods application criteria to the Forrester Agricultural Products, Inc. case study

1. The problem is serious enough to allocate the resources necessary to permanently solve and correct the problem.
    - ✓ The problem should be considered serious enough to apply this Problem-Solving approach because the reporter of the problem in this case is identified as an external customer.

2. The symptom(s) has been defined and quantified.
    - ✓ The symptom in this case was defined and quantified by the customer, although further quantification is necessary to fully understand the issue.

3. The customer who experienced the symptom(s), and other affected parties have been identified. (Customers may be internal or external).
    - ✓ Yes, the customer reported the issue.

4. Analysis of data used to define the symptom(s) demonstrate that

a nonconformance, or verified problem exists.

- ✓ The returned sample was evaluated and determined to be out of tolerance.

5. The problem is related to, (or can be reduced to), a specific occurrence.

- ✓ Based on the information, this appears to be the case.

6. Available data indicates that the problem was due to an incidence of special cause variation.

- ✓ We can assume that this incident is related to special cause variation based on the isolated nature of the problem.

Based on comparing the information from the case study to the application criteria, it is reasonable to conclude that the scenario meets the criteria to apply the 8 Step Problem Solving methodology to solve the problem.

Benchmarking

Within many organizations, there may be multiple processes where similar problems have previously occurred. Reviewing these processes and occurrences may shed light on solving this problem. Review another process and ask about the problem you are working on. Find out if they have experienced the same issue, whether they have resolved it, and if so, how?

Review the lessons learned database or the CAPA database to see if there are similar problems from the past. Find out if the problem was resolved and if so, (or if not), find out why. If there is no CAPA database or there is nothing applicable in the CAPA database, send some emails and make some phone calls. A little effort at this stage could save much more effort down the line. The point is to learn as much as you can to help your team solve the current problem. Borrow as much as possible from the work that may have already been done.

Document your benchmarking efforts and emergency responses within your Problem-Solving documentation. This includes documenting initial containment actions in a simple action plan for tracking throughout the Problem-Solving process as illustrated in Figure 2.6. The purpose for the action plan is to document and track actions taken to contain, correct, and prevent the problem. The format itself is just a matrix and the format can vary. The content is more important. In the example below from the case study, there are columns labeled as C for containment, CA for corrective action, and PA for preventive action. This makes it easy for the team to visually see that necessary consideration was given to all aspects of the problem. An action plan missing actions in any category will be lacking and generally insufficient to meet the goals of problem solving.

Emergency Action Plan

No.	Action Item	C	CA	PA	Owner	Due	Actual
1.	Issue and train affected associates in Quality Alert	X			WR	5/12/18	5/12/18
2.	Replace suspect material at customer location	X			MM	5/14/18	5/14/18
3.	Quarantine and contain/inspect all product in pipeline	X			FR	5/12/18	5/14/18
C = Containment, CA = Corrective Action, PA = Preventive Action							

Figure 2.6 Emergency Action Plan

Step 1: Pointers and Pitfalls

- Perform the necessary analysis to confirm that a nonconformance exists.

- Make sure the necessity of an Emergency Action Plan is evaluated and design an EAP that rises to the level of need in each situation.

- Use the Applications Guide to ensure a formal Problem-Solving process is necessary.

- Use the Problem-Solving Methods Guidelines to make sure this is the correct tool for the problem - using the wrong method to solve a problem may lead to poor results and recurring issues.

- Benchmark similar processes and past problem history for lessons to be learned when trying to solve a problem.
    - Failure to do this may lead to waste in terms of solving a problem that may have been solved elsewhere.

Documenting Step 1 within the 8 Step format

Problem No	Source		Line	Product Family	Part Number
051218-01	Customer – Irish Poultry Products, Inc.			Gear Box/Spur Gears	123-XYZ
	Customer reference		Qty	Date & Shift Occurred	Operation #
	N/A		1 pc	5/5/18 1st shift	Gear Mfg.
Step 2 Team Members (initials/name)		Role			
Step 3 Description of problem					
Step 4 Interim Containment actions				Assigned to	Effective Date
Step 5 Define the root cause					
Step 6 Permanent Corrective Actions - Implementation, and Validation					
Step 7 Preventive Actions - Implementation and Verification					
Step 8 Celebrate Team Success!					

Checklist	Date	Update	Date
Problem Validated?		DFMEA/PFMEA	
Containment Worksheet Completed?		Control plan(s)	
FMEA Reviewed?		Feed Across/Feed Forward	
Team includes operator?		Procedures/WI Updated	
8 Step Approved by CART?		Process Audits Implemented	
8 Step Reviewed with and presented to customer?		Training Completed	

Figure 2.7 Step 1 8-Step Report

Chapter 3

Step 2: Team Member Selection and Recruitment

The 8 Step Problem-Solving process is intended to employ a team-based structure. There are many reasons for this, but in general the idea is that the knowledge, experience, and abilities of a diverse, cross-functional team will exceed that of any individual. People from different experience levels, skill-sets, and positions will bring different strengths and perspectives and this will help to ensure that problems and solutions are reviewed from different angles and with a fresh eyes view of things.

The primary purpose of step 2 is to establish a small, cross-functional group of people with:

- the process and/or product knowledge,
- the necessary available time,
- the necessary authority,
- the necessary skillsets in the required technical disciplines to solve the problem and implement corrective actions. The team must be **Cross Functional!**

How many team members should be on a team? The number of team members varies depending on the problem and the available resources. It cannot be 1 and it should not be 20.

The problem cannot be solved by one person. The team:

- needs members with different technical skills (cross functional),
- should typically have between 4 and 7 members,
- membership can change,
- needs at least one operator, or user of the process/system,
- must be committed and available to meet regularly and to work on tasks outside of scheduled meetings as required,
- The team may want to have someone who is not technically knowledgeable of the issue, or process involved. This presents an opportunity for a "fresh eyes" perspective.

RASIC Matrix

One simple tool that can prove extremely helpful in ensuring the necessary team activities are owned by specific team members is to create a simple RASIC matrix like the one included in Figure 3.1. The RASIC matrix is helpful for defining roles and responsibilities for any activity and can be especially helpful when defining the roles and responsibilities for a team.

The acronym RASIC is defined in the legend for the matrix and the only other key to remember is that each action should only have one, (or few), owners, or person responsible. When more than one person is responsible, it often has the same effect as having nobody responsible. If you do find that your RASIC matrix has multiple owners for some of the tasks, at least reconsider the scope of and purpose for the matrix and review the degree of resolution in the matrix to see if it is narrow enough to be useful.

RASIC Matrix for Problem-Solving Team	Champion	Leader	Scribe	Timekeeper	Team Members	Process Owner
Recruit/Assign Team Members	A	R	I			C
Keep Team Focused	S	R	S	S	S	
Applying & Teaching Problem Solving	S	R				
Keeping Mtgs on Track to Time		A	S	R	S	
Provide Necessary Resources	R	S				
Manage Constraints to the Team	R	S				S
Keeping & Distributing Mtg Notes	I	A	R	I	I	
Provide Technical Input	C	A	S	S	R	C
Collect Data		A	S	S	R	S
Analyze Data	C	A	S	S	R	
Identify Solutions	C	A	S	S	R	S
Implement Solutions	I	S	S	S	S	R

Figure 3.1 RASIC Matrix for Problem-Solving Team

As a matter of instruction, the RASIC matrix is a simple X-Y matrix with the roles listed across the top of the X axis and a series of tasks, or responsibilities listed along the Y axis. The team then places the appropriate designation of responsibility in the intersecting cells. This is meant to be a very simple tool, so do not overthink it and do not get concerned over the extra time it takes to do this. The example above took 10 minutes to construct on a white board and a few minutes beyond that to put it into a spreadsheet.

The purpose for using the **RASIC** tool to identify responsibilities of team members.

R = Responsible

Those who do the work to complete the task.

A = Accountable

The one ultimately answerable for the deliverable or task.

S = Support

Provides support to the team. Helps complete the task.

I = Informed

Those who are kept up to date on progress.

C = Consulted

Those whose opinions are sought, typically subject matter experts;

Step 2 Pointers and Pitfalls

- The team needs to have a diverse skillset.
  - Members from different functions and skillsets provide a great mix of experience and ideas.
- Too few, or too many team members can impede problem solving efforts.
  - A team with too few members provides a narrow viewpoint and having too many members provides difficulty for the leader to manage.
  - The ideal and manageable team size is typically ~ 4-7 members.
- The team should always include at least one operator, or user of the process
  - The operators know more about the nuances of the process and problem than someone outside of the process will.
- When populating the RASIC matrix, you should apply "R" to only one, (or very few), team members per item. Often, if there is more than one person responsible for a task, then nobody will own the task.
- A RACI matrix is the same as the RASIC matrix without the "S",

which is used to identify the support providers for the process. My preference is to use RASIC over RACI, but do not get too hung up on the difference between the two.

Documenting Step 2 within the 8 Step format

Problem No	Source		Line	Product Family	Part Number
051218-01	Customer – Irish Poultry Products, Inc.			Gear Box/Spur Gears	123-XYZ
	Customer reference		Qty	Date & Shift Occurred	Operation #
	N/A		1 pc	5/5/18 1st shift	Gear Mfg.

Step 2 Team Members (initials/name)	Role	
T. Forrester	Champion	
F. Noe	Leader	
J. Russell	Scribe	
H. Wheatley	Timekeeper	
D. Pickerell	Team Member	
C. Morris	Process Owner	

Step 3 Description of problem

Step 4 Interim Containment actions	Assigned to	Effective Date

Step 5 Define the root cause

Step 6 Permanent Corrective Actions - Implementation, and Validation

Step 7 Preventive Actions - Implementation and Verification

Step 8 Celebrate Team Success!

Checklist		Date	Update		Date
Problem Validated?			DFMEA/PFMEA		
Containment Worksheet Completed?			Control plan(s)		
FMEA Reviewed?			Feed Across/Feed Forward		
Team includes operator?			Procedures/WI Updated		
8 Step Approved by CART?			Process Audits Implemented		
8 Step Reviewed with and presented to customer?			Training Completed		

Figure 3.2 Step 2 8-Step Report

Chapter 4

Step 3: Problem Statement

The purpose for step 3 is to clearly describe the problem to be solved. The goal for step 3 is to create a detailed, yet concise problem statement that answers what is wrong with what? The importance of a properly written problem statement cannot be overstated. A well-written problem statement will help to provide context and scope regarding the problem the team is trying to solve. When done correctly, it will provide enough detail to establish necessary boundaries and direction for the team through the rest of the

Problem-Solving process. In this chapter we will prepare a problem definition and a problem description and will combine them to create a useful problem statement.

The problem definition is simply defining the problem in terms of a deviation from the requirement, or standard. What is a problem? A problem is the difference between what should be happening and what is happening. The problem represents a gap in performance.

It is not hyperbole to say that the success of the Problem-Solving effort is largely dependent on properly preparing the problem statement. John Dewey's quote about this, "A problem well-defined is a problem half-solved" is more true than it is hyperbole.

A Problem Statement is a simple, yet detailed statement that describes the defect, or failure for which the cause is unknown. Remember what Albert Einstein said about this, "If you cannot say it simply, you do not understand the problem". A well stated Problem Statement answers the question **"What is wrong with what?"**

The purpose of the Problem Statement is to:
1. Provide a starting point for understanding the problem,
2. Keep the team focused and aligned,
3. Define and narrow the scope of the root cause analysis.

Question: How can the Problem Statement help to keep the team focused?

Answer: Problem solving teams can easily get side-tracked and the team leader must constantly re-focus the team on the problem at hand, as defined by the problem statement.

Question: How can the Problem Statement help to narrow the scope of the RCA?

Answer: The proper degree of specificity in the problem statement is critical to defining the scope of the activities of the team. Solving a problem in the "Machining Department" is much different in scope than solving a problem from "Line 3" in the Machining Department.

It is critical for the Problem-Solving team to go through the necessary steps to arrive at the correct problem description. Some teams fail to do this, relying instead on transferring the issue description that is presented to them by the affected party. This may be from a customer, (internal, or external), an auditor, or some other affected party. Please remember that people who are affected by the issue likely do not know enough about your process to communicate an accurate idea about the problem and are simply reporting the symptoms that they experience, often doing so in vague statements.

The steps to developing an effective problem statement:

1. Communicate with the Problem-Solving team about the importance of the problem statement for the success of the Problem-Solving effort.
2. Review with the team all the information currently known about the problem.
3. Lead the team to complete the 5W2H exercise.
4. Use the information from the 5W2H exercise to construct the problem statement. This may take some trial and error and some modifications as it is not an exact science.

    Note: It is not a requirement to use all the information. The Team Leader should lead the team to determine which of information from the answers is most relevant and construct the problem statement from that information.

5. Review and revise the problem statement until it meets the previously stated criteria:

    o A Simple yet detailed statement that describes the defect, or failure and answers the question, what is wrong with what?

5W2H Matrix

The 5W2H is an acronym for who, what, when, where, why, how many, and how big? The purpose for and the value of the 5W2H tool is to ask the right questions to be able to establish boundaries around the initial understanding of the problem. The answers to the 7 questions provide the necessary details to allow the team to create the boundaries around describing the problem. This makes it a perfect tool to use for preparing the problem statement.

I prefer this tool for helping to create a problem statement because it helps to narrow the focus of the problem. In practice, each of the 7 words has questions to be answered about the initial understanding of the problem. The questions can vary and can be customized by different organizations. Some of the important nuances for this tool include knowing that it is ok to not answer all the questions if the answers are truly unknown and the answers are not available with some initial investigation. Another thing to note is that when answering about why, do not start down the path of trying to explain the root cause of the problem in this step. The cause cannot be answered yet and this would beg the team to start guessing, which is not part of the path to successful Problem Solving.

	Questions	Answers
Who?	Who reported the problem?	
	Who is affected by the problem?	
What?	What has been reported as the problem?	
When?	When was the problem first experienced?	
	When was it first reported?	
Where?	Where was the problem first experienced?	
	Where on the part was the problem?	
Why?	Why is this a problem?	
How many?	How many occurrences/units are involved?	
How big?	How big is the deviation from the requirement?	

Figure 4.1 5W2H Matrix

5W2H Matrix for Forrester Agricultural Products, Inc. Case Study

	Questions	Answers
Who?	Who reported the problem?	Irish Poultry Products, Inc.
	Who is affected by the problem?	Irish Poultry Products, Inc.
What?	What has been reported as the problem?	Part number 123/XY Z Creating noise in poultry feeder
When?	When was the problem first experienced?	May 12, 2018 at 3:47 PM
	When was it first reported?	May 12, 2018 at 3:47 PM
Where?	Where was the problem first experienced?	Irish Poultry Products, Inc.
	Where on the part was the problem?	Gear Teeth contact surface
Why?	Why is this a problem?	The noise in the feeder distracted the chickens from eating
How many?	How many occurrences/units are involved?	1 pc
How big?	How big is the deviation from the requirement?	The noise level exceeded the design spec by 2.1dB

Figure 4.2 Completed 5W2H Matrix

Once the team has completed the 5W2H matrix based on all available information, the team must decide which information is most relevant to use for constructing the problem statement. While there is no perfect answer to what the problem description should look like, it must be a simple, yet detailed statement that describes the defect or failure and answers what is wrong with what. Please review a couple of examples of problem statements based on the FAPI case study and see if those items are addressed.

Problem Statement Example 1

"The customer reported a problem with the chicken feeder."

Problem Statement Example 2

"The customer reported noise and vibration in the chicken feeder."

Are these good problem statements? Why, or why not? Neither statement provides enough information to truly understand the problem and both look like symptoms as reported by the affected party. There is not enough detail in these statements to be able to help guide the team.

Problem Statement Example 3

"On May 12, 2018, Irish Poultry Products, Inc. reported 1 gearbox of P/N 123-XYZ produced on May 5, 2018, with excessive noise due to dents/dings on gear teeth contact surfaces."

Does this example look like a reasonable problem statement? Why, or why not?

While the problem statement in the above example can certainly be critiqued to some degree, it does accomplish the objectives that we previously established.

- It is a simple yet detailed statement that describes the defect, or failure.
- It does answer what is wrong with what.

Based on the information in problem statement example 3, we know what the part is, what the part feature is, when the part was produced, where it was produced, and for whom it was produced. Remember the John Dewey quote we discussed previously, "A problem well-defined is a problem half-solved". This problem statement is sufficiently detailed in that it serves to reduce the scope of the Problem-Solving focus to a nearly pinpoint level of detail. Knowing what part is involved removes the focus from other parts. Knowing what part feature is involved removes the focus from other part features. Knowing which production process the part was produced on removes the need to focus on other production lines. With this problem description, we can create a very specific and narrowly focused Problem-Solving scope. This aligns very well with the intent of the Dewey quote.

As we previously discussed, a well-defined problem statement must be narrow in scope to help take a large issue and narrow the focus to a more manageable problem. Do not try to solve expansive, or global issues with this process. Instead, when faced with a problem with multiple occurrences, focus on solving one representative, recent problem and then work to feed forward and feed across the countermeasures to the rest of the like issues. In other words, do not try to eat the entire elephant at once.

It is important to mention that while the examples on the previous page point to individual parts produced in a manufacturing process, the same tools and methods can be used in a variety of industries and processes. I have personally applied the same methods to create problem statements for safety incidents, financial and transactional processes, and from multiple industries ranging from automotive, to building supplies, and fiber optic cable systems.

Another thing to point out in the example problem statement is that it refers to "excessive noise due to dents/dings on gear teeth contact surfaces". Even though the problem statement talks about the noise being due to dents and dings on the gear teeth, it is not assigning the root cause as we still do not know why there are dents/dings. That level of detail, however, does greatly narrow the scope of the problem to be solved.

Step 3 Pointers and Pitfalls

- The problem statement must answer what is wrong with what.
- The problem statement is foundational for the directional alignment of the Problem-Solving team going forward.
- The problem statement must be detailed and specific to narrow the scope of the Problem-Solving process.
- The problem statement should not include perceived root causes or corrective actions as these items have not yet been determined.

Documenting Step 3 within the 8 Step format

Problem No	Source		Line	Product Family	Part Number
051218-01	Customer – Irish Poultry Products, Inc.			Gear Box/Spur Gears	123-XYZ
	Customer reference		Qty	Date & Shift Occurred	Operation #
	N/A		1 pc	5/5/18 1st shift	Gear Mfg.

Step 2 Team Members (initials/name)	Role
T. Forrester	Champion
F. Noe	Leader
J. Russell	Scribe
H. Wheatley	Timekeeper
D. Pickerell	Team Member
C. Morris	Process Owner

Step 3 Description of problem

On May 12, 2018, Irish Poultry Products, Inc. reported 1 gearbox of P/N 123-XYZ produced on May 5, 2018, with excessive noise due to dents/dings on gear teeth contact surface .

Step 4 Interim Containment actions	Assigned to	Effective Date

Step 5 Define the root cause

Step 6 Permanent Corrective Actions - Implementation, and Validation

Step 7 Preventive Actions - Implementation and Verification

Step 8 Celebrate Team Success!

Checklist	Date	Update	Date
Problem Validated?		DFMEA/PFMEA	
Containment Worksheet Completed?		Control plan(s)	
FMEA Reviewed?		Feed Across/Feed Forward	
Team includes operator?		Procedures/WI Updated	
8 Step Approved by CART?		Process Audits Implemented	
8 Step Reviewed with and presented to customer?		Training Completed	

Figure 4.3 Step 3 8-Step Report

Chapter 5

Step 4: Containment & Interim Corrective Actions

The sophistication of containment actions may vary depending on the impact and risk level of the problem, (the team will need to determine this). **Assuming the risk warrants it**, what containment means to me is "not one more". What I am really asking for, (or expecting), is that a robust enough containment activity be put in place that there is not one more issue related to the current problem that gets through the process unintended. Some people see this as a safety net to protect the customer from another defect and some people see it as an impenetrable wall that nothing unintended can get through and they might even refer to this as a "Quality Wall".

The need for robust containment is sometimes not taken seriously enough. This is often due to either a lack of understanding of the benefits, or due to the disdain for the wasteful expense of containment that is incurred by the owner of the process. Understanding the wasteful cost should drive more thorough and urgent root cause analysis and implementation and validation of permanent corrective actions so the cost can be mitigated as soon as it is safe to do so. Remember, the only thing costlier than doing extra containment activities is not doing them and burdening the customer with recurring problems.

Interim Corrective Actions are also sometimes called Temporary Corrective Actions, Temporary Countermeasures, or Containment Actions. Interim Corrective Actions are actions that are intended to detect the defect or raise awareness of the issue(s) until Permanent Corrective Actions are implemented **and** verified. The purpose is to define, verify and implement the Containment Action to isolate the effects of the problem from any internal/external customer until permanent corrective actions are implemented and validated for effectiveness.

An Interim Corrective Action:
- ✓ Addresses symptoms.
- ✓ Is verified for effectiveness.
- ✓ Is monitored while being used.
- ✓ Is documented.
- ✓ Adds cost.
- ✓ Is temporary.
- ✓ Is later replaced by Permanent Corrective Action.

Interim Corrective Actions may include:
- ✓ Additional inspection of product prior to shipping it.
- ✓ A Quality Alert.

- ✓ A Safety Alert to heighten awareness of the issue.
- ✓ Recalling, or retrieving product that has already been shipped.
- ✓ A temporary additional process step.

Affected employees need to be trained in the ICA and the training should be documented. The actions themselves should be documented with a brief description of the ICA, who owns it, date opened, and date closed.

Steps to Identify and Implement Temporary Corrective Actions

1. Review all available information regarding the problem including customer(s) involved, (if applicable), processes involved, and products or outputs involved.
2. Use the information from step 1 to make sure you understand the reported issue and potential impacts. See if there could be other products or processes not initially included in the problem that should be included in the containment.
3. Review the results from the Emergency Actions taken in Problem Solving Step 1 from Chapter 2.
4. Verify whether other customers or locations receive the same product or service. If so, determine whether a proactive containment for those products/locations is warranted.
5. Review, (or create if necessary), a simple process map to show the overall linear flow of the process and where the issue occurred.
6. Use the process map from step 5 to visually understand where in the process the problem occurred and where there may be areas impacted by the problem. This information can help to point the team to where additional containment steps may be needed.
7. Develop and validate the containment actions. Validation is a critical step to ensuring the containment will effectively protect the customer, (or downstream processes), from being further impacted. Whenever possible, ensure containment activities are conducted

outside of the normal process flow. Expecting a process user or operator to doublecheck their own work and calling this containment does not meet the intent of "not one more".

8. Train all process users of the containment activities. Document the training.
9. Document the containment actions on the action plan for the problem. (See Figure 5.1.)
10. Report on the containment results. The results should be visible at the point of containment and should be compiled and distributed to necessary parties. Determine whether the customer requires or is interested in periodic containment results updates.
11. Audit the containment activities. Add this to Layered Process Audits, or implement special audits to ensure the instructions, training, and quarantine activities are being followed and maintained.
12. Meet regularly to review the results and to determine if different or additional steps are needed.
13. Remove containment actions only after permanent corrective and preventive actions have been implemented and validated as effective.

Action Plan

Document all containment actions on the action plan, (see example in Figure 5.1). The action plan is a simple register of all actions taken to contain and correct the problem. The action plan lists the actions to be taken, the owner, due date, and the type of action in terms of whether it is a containment action, corrective action, or preventive action. Identifying the type of action is a simple step, but it is useful in doing a sanity check regarding whether all types of actions were considered when addressing the problem.

No.	Action Item	C	CA	PA	Owner	Due	Actual
1.	Issue and train affected associates in Quality Alert	X			WR	5/12/18	5/12/18
2.	Replace suspect material at customer location	X			MM	5/14/18	5/14/18
3.	Quarantine and contain/inspect all product in pipeline	X			FR	5/12/18	5/14/18
4.	Implement interim requirement for Supervisor to review and sign-off all tool changes until Perm CA implemented	X			WR	5/13/18	5/13/18
5.	Feed Across containment actions to the other production processes	X			WR	5/13/18	5/13/18
6.	Train operators and supervisors in actions #4 and 5.	X			WR	5/13/18	5/13/18

C = Containment, CA = Corrective Action, PA = Preventive Action

Figure 5.1 Containment Action Plan

Step 4 Pointers and Pitfalls

&⌐ Interim Corrective Actions are used to mitigate the symptoms and effects of a problem before permanent corrective actions can be implemented or validated.

&⌐ ICAs are costly and should only be implemented on a temporary basis.

&⌐ Employees who are affected and responsible for the ICAs must receive formal, documented training on the ICAs.

&⌐ ICA effectiveness and continued implementation must be monitored, and results documented.

Documenting Step 4 within the 8 Step format

Problem No	Source		Line	Product Family	Part Number
051218-01	Customer – Irish Poultry Products, Inc.			Gear Box/Spur Gears	123-XYZ
	Customer reference		Qty	Date & Shift Occurred	Operation #
	N/A		1 pc	5/5/18 1st shift	Gear Mfg.

Step 2 Team Members (initials/name)	Role
T. Forrester	Champion
F. Noe	Leader
J. Russell	Scribe
H. Wheatley	Timekeeper
D. Pickerell	Team Member
C. Morris	Process Owner

Step 3 Description of problem

On May 12, 2018, Irish Poultry Products, Inc. reported 1 gearbox of P/N 123-XYZ produced on May 5, 2018, with excessive noise due to dents/dings on gear teeth contact surface .

Step 4 Interim Containment actions	Assigned to	Effective Date
See attached Action Plan		

Step 5 Define the root cause

Step 6 Permanent Corrective Actions - Implementation, and Validation

Step 7 Preventive Actions - Implementation and Verification

Step 8 Celebrate Team Success!

Checklist	Date	Update	Date
Problem Validated?		DFMEA/PFMEA	
Containment Worksheet Completed?		Control plan(s)	
FMEA Reviewed?		Feed Across/Feed Forward	
Team includes operator?		Procedures/WI Updated	
8 Step Approved by CART?		Process Audits Implemented	
8 Step Reviewed with and presented to customer?		Training Completed	

Figure 5.2 Step 4 8-Step Report

Chapter 6

Step 5: Root Cause Analysis

What is a Root Cause? A root cause should be considered to be "a cause, that if altered or removed, would have either eliminated or substantially altered the outcome." There are two questions to ask if you are unsure whether you have found a root cause:

1. Would the event have occurred if this cause had not been present?
2. Will the problem recur if this cause is corrected or eliminated?

The root cause is the primary reason, or reasons, a problem occurs. When problems have been "solved" and they continue to recur, it is often because the true root cause(s) were never identified or corrected. Problems often have more than one contributing root cause, or *potential* root cause.

What is not a root cause? A root cause is not a symptom, it is not a source, it is not a causal factor, it is not in and of itself correlation, and it is not a person.

Is it a symptom, or a root cause?

A symptom is an indication of a problem. It is like the tip of an iceberg being visible above the water but knowing that the majority of it is beneath the surface and not visible at first glance, or a tree with the roots extending far below the surface of the ground. The symptom is the visible, or exposed result of a problem. Symptoms include things like, "it does not fit", "it is the wrong part", "it does not look good", "it is noisy", etc. The symptom is typically what is reported by the customer or affected party regarding a problem they are experiencing. The actual root cause can typically only be defined through some investigation and a focused, disciplined root cause analysis.

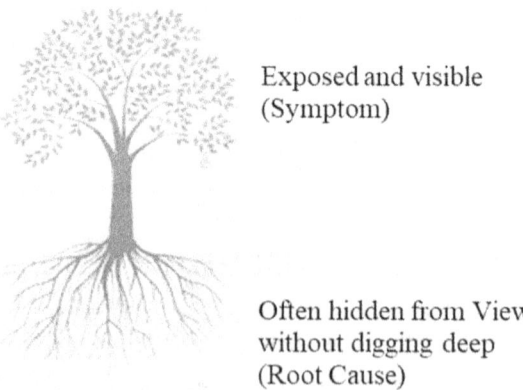

Exposed and visible (Symptom)

Often hidden from View without digging deep (Root Cause)

Figure 6.1 Root Cause Analogy

The Root Cause, or a Source?

The root cause of a problem and the source of the problem are not the same thing, so do not confuse the two. Toyota's Taiichi Ohno talked about focusing on identifying the true root cause of a problem and said that "the root cause lies hidden beyond the source", (Liker, 258). The source of a problem may be a tool, a process, a supplier, etc. Knowing the source of a problem is important, but it does not explain *why*.

The Owl Approach to Problem Solving

Far too many root cause analyses begin and end with who. "Who didn't follow the process?" Who didn't catch the defect in inspection?" Whose fault is it?" After leading Problem-Solving teams and teaching Problem-Solving training courses for over 25 years, I can state that far more times than not it is not the process user's fault for causing the problem.

If the Problem-Solving activities do point to issues where employees failed to do what was required and what they were trained to do, then, if necessary, the applicable leadership must deal with that issue as an issue that is separate from the Problem-Solving team. Personnel issues cannot be managed by the Problem-Solving team.

Focus on the Process when Looking for the Root Cause

A process is a series of sequential steps that are executed to complete a specific activity. A process starts with an input that goes through a series of activities and ends with an output. People often think of processes as being manufacturing processes, but there are also many other types of support, service, and transactional business processes. It does not matter what type of process it is, whether it is a manufacturing process, a support process, or a transactional process, ***"Make the Root Cause Analysis about the process"***. Instead of asking questions about ***Who caused this***, we should be asking questions about ***Why the process failed*** and focusing on the process and systems.

This is an important point to spend a little time focusing on because it is a common failure in many "Problem-Solving" applications. I have seen many cases where the root cause presented was "operator error". If you play that scenario out to the end, it is likely to conclude with some "corrective action" like; counselled the operator or disciplined the operator. This is typically followed with operator re-training, which usually leads me to the conclusion that the operator must not have been trained in the first place because they still "failed". If they were trained and still failed, then how does re-training the operator solve the issue and prevent recurrence? My comments about this should not be confused to imply that we should not train our operators relative to corrective actions, of course we should. Especially once the real root cause and corrective and preventive actions are determined and implemented.

Whenever I see a root cause pointing to operator error, I try to remind people of what Dr. Deming said: "A bad system will beat a good person every time". I always ask this about operator error: **"what about the process allowed, or caused the operator to err?"**

This is not meant to imply that leaders who do this are bad people who go out of their way to blame their employees. This type of leadership usually stems from poorly trained leaders who are themselves often the result of a culture that was created by poor leaders. Poor leadership begets poor leadership.

In some extreme cases, this type of reaction from leadership comes from a culture that is built around blame and punishment and it becomes the dominant force within the culture. John Lee refers to one characteristic of poor leadership culture as "PBP", which is Personify, Blame, and Punish, (Lee, 2012). If the goal in root cause analysis is to identify the true root cause(s), then focusing on who to blame is not going to get to the desired result.

There are some examples of employees overriding, or ignoring a well-designed, presented, and trained process, but that conclusion should be rare and as a last resort after carefully examining the process objectively. If your Pareto chart of "causes" looks like the one in Figure 6.2, your organization has much bigger issues than whatever issues the employees are or are not causing.

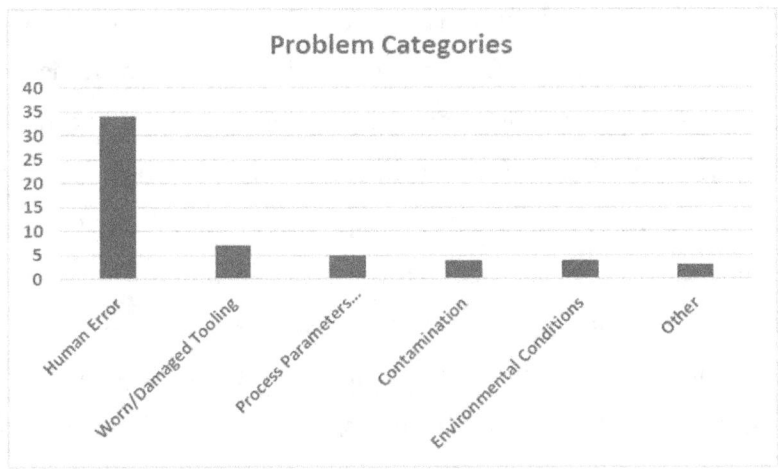

Figure 6.2 Problem Categories (Example)

The Root Cause Analysis must be Intentional and Focused

Part of what is meant by "taking the root cause analysis seriously", is not jumping to, or accepting from others, a quick diagnosis of the root cause of a problem that was previously vetted as being serious enough to spend time solving. Not taking the root cause analysis seriously is often characterized by presenting what someone *thinks* or *feels* about the root cause. These things are important and necessary when brainstorming, but the root cause is not presented based solely on the results of brainstorming.

The Root Cause Analysis, (RCA), is one of the most important steps to Problem Solving. For a variety of reasons, RCA is also one of the most overlooked steps. How can the Root Cause Analysis be overlooked when it is obviously integral to the Problem-Solving process? This happens for several reasons, most of which are related to relying on experience versus empirical evidence specific to current problem. One of the reasons organizations do not follow a structured approach to root cause analysis is because someone already *knows* the answers. "I already know the Root Cause because I have solved this problem several times before". Sound familiar?

Another failure to follow a disciplined approach to Root Cause Analysis is caused by reliance on the **Jury of Executive Opinion**. Root cause analysis by The Jury of Executive Opinion occurs when a group of leaders get together and provide some anecdotal cause(s) for a problem. The Jury of Executive Opinion often provides a response much like the following, "based on our collective and extensive experience, we feel like the likely root cause is this…". Whenever the root cause is mentioned in the same statement with someone's feelings, be cautious.

The "Problem-Solving" method known as **Trial and Error** is yet another excuse to not follow a disciplined approach for Root Cause Analysis. The Trial-and-Error approach includes implementing multiple changes on a process, product, or system to affect the outcome without really knowing which changes lead to the improvement. This approach is wasteful and typically relies on luck to figure out how to improve some condition without fully understanding the cause(s) for a problem. I am not saying that this is not how problems sometimes get solved, but without the presence of some structured Problem-Solving activity, I would be very skeptical.

Root Cause Categories

There are three primary categories of Root Causes for the shipment of nonconforming product, or the performance of a nonconforming service:

1. Why Made? (Occurrence)
2. Why Shipped? (Detection)
3. Why the System Failed? (Systemic)

The leader of a Problem-Solving team must ensure that the team stays focused on the issue they are solving. The team cannot confuse one root cause category with another. (Note: it is important to note that "shipment of nonconforming products" does not have to apply only to those products shipped outside the organization. The same idea of "Why Shipped?" can also be applied to an occurrence of a product or transaction leaving one process and going to another. The problem of shipping, or transferring, the output still occurred and the root cause analysis for why shipped should still be analyzed and corrected.)

Specific Root Cause: The **Specific** root cause is the root cause that focuses on why the specific nonconformance occurred. The specific root cause typically includes the identification of a change point. We will refer to this as "Why Made?"

The Why Made root cause category is used for understanding why a defect was made, or why an error occurred. Example: The root cause for why made is not because the operator did not inspect the part. It must be about *why* the process yielded the defect.

Detection Root Cause: The **Detection** root cause is the root cause that focuses on why the specific defect escaped detection. We will refer to this as "Why Not Detected?" The Why Not Detected root cause category is used for understanding why and how a defect got out of the process. How did the inspection process fail?

Some examples of root causes for Why Not Detected:

- Process is not looking for it, (it is not a required inspection)
- Tools/methods not in place, (there is no method for inspection)
- Tools/methods in place, but inadequate, (the tools provided are inadequate for detection)
- Not following the control plan (Inspection), (not conducting the required inspections, or at the required frequency)
- Not following the control plan (Reaction)
- Bypassed Detection/Mistake Proofing tools
- Escaped (the defect was detected but placed back into product flow)

Systemic Root Cause: The **Systemic** root cause is the root cause that focuses on why the system failed to prevent the failure. Systemic root causes often pertain to why the Quality System failed, (poor NPI process, Gage Calibration Process, Design Control, etc.)

Understanding Change Points

When trying to find the root cause of a problem, it is important to understand that what we are often dealing with is a specific point of change, (or change point), as we briefly discussed in chapter 2. The concept of a change point can be simply characterized as a process that was operating at a specific level and then some change was introduced that in turn, changed the result or output. Identifying a process change point will not necessarily identify the root cause, but it can help to lead the team in the right direction.

Types of Change Points

When considering change points in most processes, there are generally 2 primary categories: planned and unplanned. Planned, (or known), changes often include things like planned maintenance activity, tooling changes, process physics changes, equipment programming changes, planned material changes, supplier changes, and operator changes. Unplanned changes often include things like breakdowns, unplanned equipment changes, emergency operator changes, unplanned changes to materials, unplanned changes by suppliers, and environmental changes such as temperature, vibration, humidity, contamination, etc. While this does not represent an exhaustive list of all possible process changes, it does provide an example of changes that are common and typical, especially in a manufacturing process.

Identifying the Change Point

The approach taken to identifying the change points in a process can vary depending on the culture of the organization as well as the experience of the Problem-Solving team leader. This is true because some organizations have a disciplined approach to process management and change management when compared to other organizations. If an organization is not disciplined and structured around change management, then it is common for well-intended changes to take place that are not always fully communicated, validated, or documented.

The following is a series of typical steps to take when trying to identify a change point within a process:

1. Try to pinpoint the approximate time that the problem occurred. This will require revisiting the details from the earlier investigation.
2. Based on the best available information from step 1, interview the area supervisors, operators, maintenance techs to check their knowledge of any processes changes around the timeframe identified.
3. Again, based on the best available information from step 1, review all available records to identify specific changes such as maintenance records, change logs, process logs, staffing rosters, training records, inspection records, Lean Daily Management/Lean Tier boards, and data logged within process equipment.
4. Use the information learned and try to assemble a timeline of actions and changes from before the known problem occurred until it was found.

Identifying the Root Cause(s)

There are numerous tools and methods that can be used to determine the root cause(s) of a problem. For the purposes of this book, we will focus on a few that have proven to be particularly useful. The list presented below includes an 8-step process for conducting a root cause analysis. The steps are numbered 1 through 8 because they are intended to be linear and completed in the order in which they appear. There are many mistakes that people make in their Problem-Solving efforts by relying on any one of the steps below as the beginning and end of their Root Cause Analysis efforts. This often leads to poor root cause analysis and resulting Problem Solving, which in turn leads to recurring issues, and wasted time and money.

List of Common Steps for Conducting a Root Cause Analysis

1. Review the problem statement.
2. Review relevant data and information.
3. **Go to the process**! Observe the process in operation, the material

flow, the process steps, the process layouts, the operator movements, how parts are staged, etc.
4. Interview process experts: Operators, Process Users, Team Leaders, Supervisors, Proc Eng., etc.
5. Brainstorming: Identify as many potential causes as possible.
6. Fishbone Diagram: Organize and determine most likely issues (Utilize multi-voting, or Nominal Group Technique, if necessary, to determine the most likely issues)
7. 5-Why Analysis: Determine likely root cause(s).
8. Return to process: Initiate the failure mode if possible/practical Try to turn the cause on and off to re-create the defect/failure.

Detailed Common Steps for Conducting a Root Cause Analysis

1. Review the Problem Statement

As we previously discussed, reviewing the problem statement is an important step to conducting a root cause analysis. Reviewing the problem statement will help the team focus on the problem they are solving. This prevents the team from getting sidetracked with other issues that come to light during the process. A helpful hint here is for the leader to write the problem statement in the corner of the whiteboard, or on a flip chart, for the team to see and review throughout the process. The problem statement from the FAPI case study appears below:

"On May 12, 2018, Forrester Agricultural Products, Inc. reported 1 gearbox of P/N 123-XYZ produced on May 5, 2018, with excessive noise due to dents/dings on gear teeth contact surface."

2. Review relevant data and information

Keep relevant, known information available to the team. Again, I would recommend writing this on a whiteboard so that it is visible during the process. Relevant, known data may include the following:

o   Information reported by the customer in the nonconformance notification.

o   Information obtained during the initial investigation.

o   Information collected during containment actions.

Another item that was deemed to be very important to the Problem-Solving team in this case was a review of the process map for the gear manufacturing process. The team reviewed the process map to help them plan for what they needed to see during the Problem-Solving process.

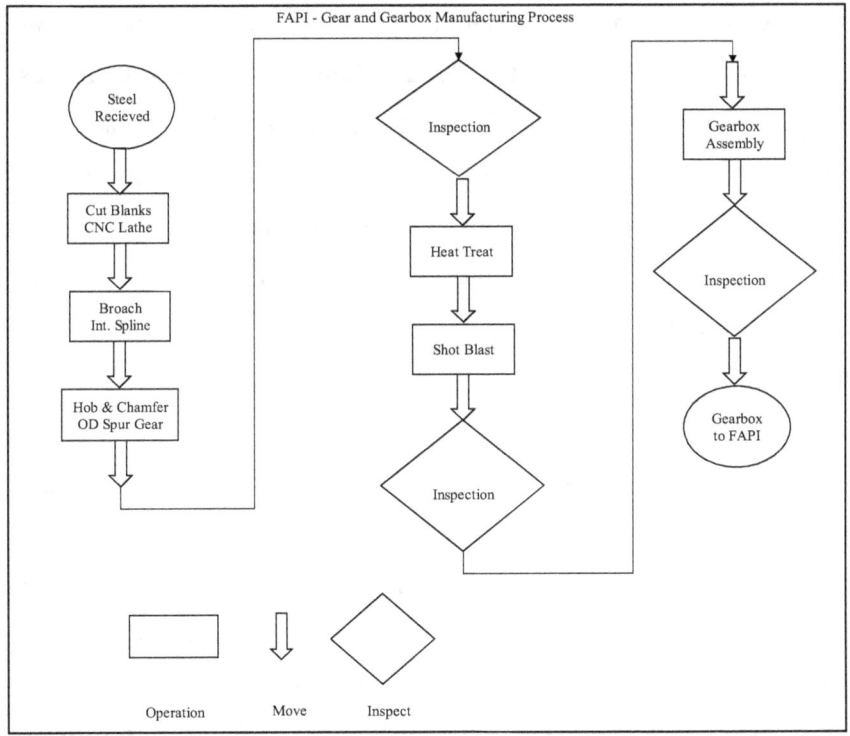

Figure 6.3 FAPI Process Map

3. Go to the Process!

Toyota's Nampachi Hayashi stressed the need to go to the process when he said, "use your feet to investigate processes and not your computer", (Liker, 262). The Japanese refer to this as Gemba, which roughly translated into English means, "the actual place". The main purpose for this step is to see first-hand what goes on in the process. This is where the nuances of what happens versus what is supposed to happen are learned. The team cannot gain a high enough level of understanding of a problem in a process without seeing the process. This step is sometimes skipped by new, or inexperienced leaders who do not know that the conference room is not where the real Problem Solving takes place.

4. **Interview process experts**

During the visit to Gemba, it is important to talk with the people most familiar with the process. By "most familiar with the process", I am talking about the people who are the most familiar with how the process is *supposed* to function well as the people who are most familiar with how the process actually *does* function. Operators, supervisors, maintenance techs, and other users of the process know more about the day-to-day issues and nuances of the process. The Engineers who designed and installed the process know more about how the process was intended to function before wear and tear took affect and before workarounds were added.

5. **Brainstorming**

Brainstorming Process

There are numerous approaches to brainstorming and most experienced Problem-Solving leaders have their favorite or go-to method. Various methods include the Round Robin approach where team members write an idea on a card and pass it to the next person. They see what was written and they add their idea. This continues until there are no more ideas to write.

Another method is the Crawford Slip method. The Crawford Slip method begins with a team review of the Problem Description and then the team members write their ideas on individual sticky notes, or cards and give them to the facilitator for consolidation.

The method that seems to be used very often and is easy to use is a simple free-for-all approach where the team reviews the Problem Description and then randomly says their ideas if they have any and the facilitator records the ideas. Although this process usually takes just a few minutes, some leaders like to apply a time limit to the activity. I have not found it necessary to put a time limit on the activity, but I will put a secret time limit of 1 minute on the max amount of time since the last new idea. I will not share this ahead of time because I do not want to constrict the creativity of the team, but if there is not a new idea in 1 minute, the team is likely done.

There are pros and cons to each method. For example, the Round Robin method forces a team member to try to come up with something to write, which may cause some anxiety and inhibit free-thinking. The Crawford Slip method provides some degree of anonymity but takes a little more work for the facilitator. The Free-for-all approach is quick and easy but does not provide anonymity.

Conducting a Free-For-All Brainstorming approach can be accomplished in the following steps:

1. Define and agree to the objective.
2. Review the Problem Description to refresh the parameters for the team.
3. Brainstorm ideas and suggestions.
   (A time limit is generally not necessary when doing a free-for-all approach as the facilitator needs to know to stop it when the flow of ideas stops, which typically takes no more than a few minutes.)
4. The facilitator, or scribe will record the ideas on a flipchart, or whiteboard.
5. Categorize/condense/combine/refine the ideas.

Brainstorming List from Forrester Agricultural Products, Inc. Case Study

> May 16, 2018
>
> Forrester Agricultural Products – Chicken Feeder Problem Statement
>
> Brainstorming List
> - Parts were dropped
> - Parts were damaged in hobbing process
> - Parts were damaged during inspection
> - Parts were damaged while being moved
> - Parts were damaged during assembly
> - Parts were damaged during broaching
> - Parts were damaged during loading onto racks
> - Operator not trained
> - Operator failed to follow process
> - Parts being hit at the process during maintenance activities
> - Metals shavings pressed into gear while clamping
>
> "On May 12, 2018, Forrester Agricultural Products, Inc. reported 1 gearbox of P/N 123-XYZ produced on May 5, 2018, with excessive noise due to dents/dings on gear teeth contact surface"

Figure 6.4 Brainstorming List

Once you have generated ideas and have eliminated the far-fetched, non-sensical ideas, it is a good idea to organize the remaining ideas on a Fishbone Diagram.

6. **Fishbone Diagram (Cause and Effect Diagram)**
    1. Enter the problem statement in the box at the right.
    2. Enter the ideas on the diagram under the appropriate category.
    3. Once all ideas are entered, see if the team can come up with additional ideas based on the ideas listed and enter them on branches coming off the original ideas.
    4. Once any additional ideas are entered, begin to narrow them down by likelihood of occurrence. Strikethrough the ideas that are most unlikely, but do not erase those ideas as they may be

reviewed again later.
5. Next, categorize the remaining ideas by each of the three legs of the root cause analysis, as appropriate.
6. Once all remaining ideas are categorized for the root cause analysis, move onto the 5-Why Analysis.

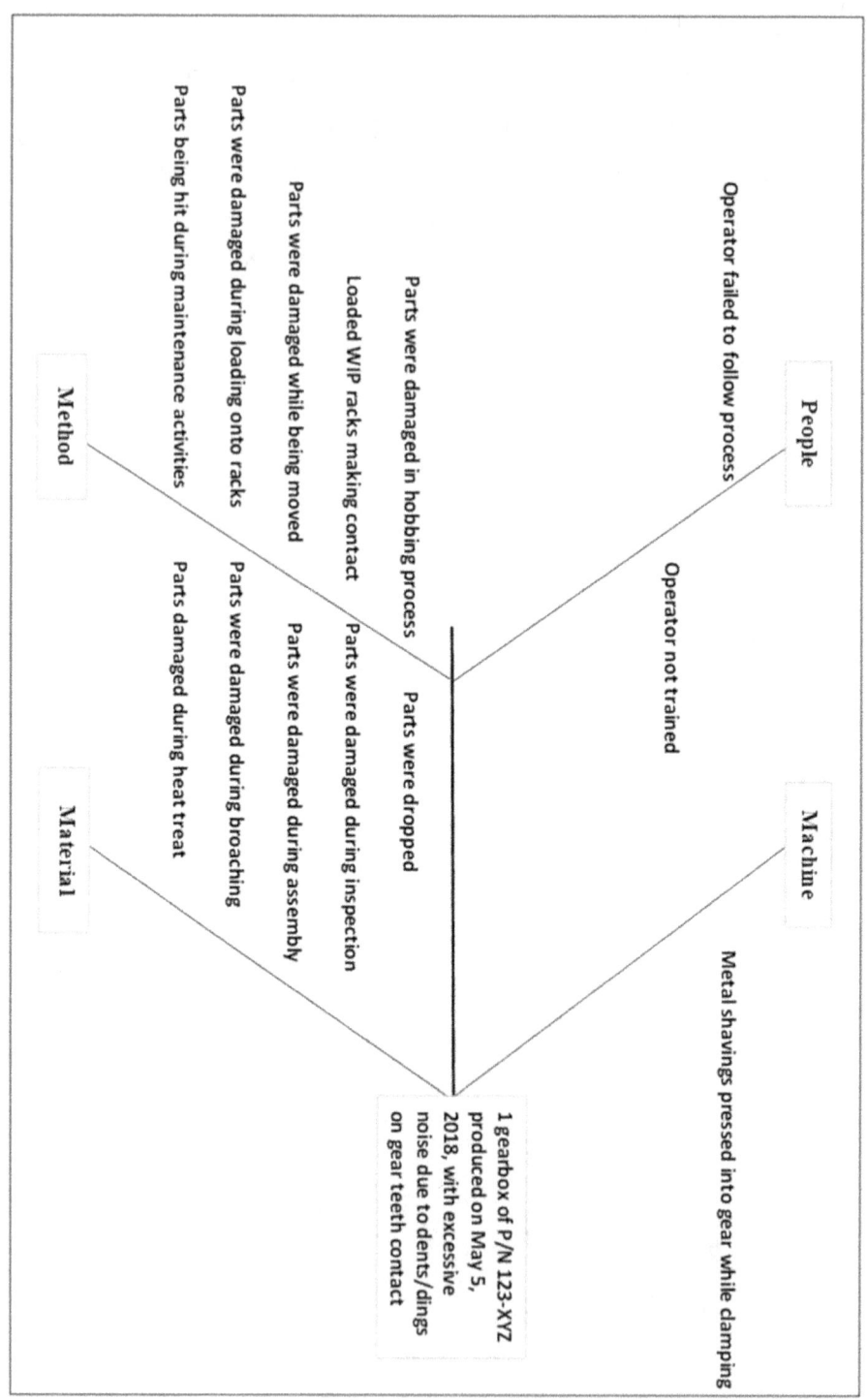

Figure 6.5 Fishbone Diagram 1

Now that the Fishbone Diagram has been constructed by populating it with the ideas from the brainstorming session, the team will once again review it for any possible piggy-back ideas that may stem from seeing an idea and triggering a new idea with someone.

For the next step, after reviewing the completed diagram, the team narrowed the list of potential causes by circling only those items that would apply to the gears becoming damaged on the gear teeth and only for the why made part of the Root Cause Analysis.

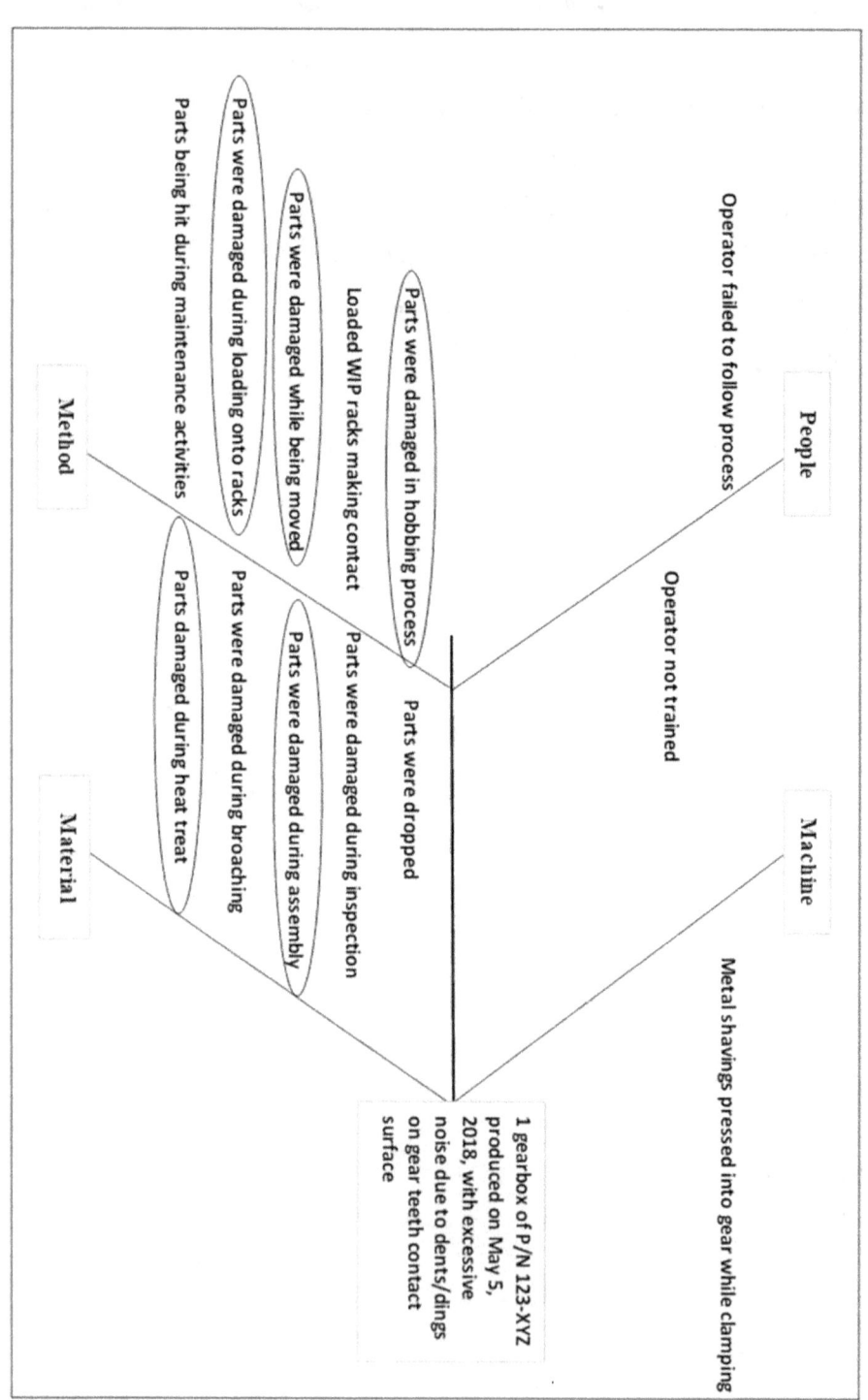

Figure 6.6 Fishbone Diagram 2

Which Potential Cause to Pursue?

Once the team has completed the Fishbone Diagram, there may be multiple potential causes. The team cannot effectively chase after more than one potential cause at the same time, so it will be necessary to prioritize the potential causes to enable focus on one at a time based on the team's collective prioritization.

As I had previously mentioned, at the conclusion of the fishbone exercise you may find that there are multiple causes to drill down using the 5 Why analysis tool. How do you choose one to pursue? There are several tools to use to help select which causes to pursue including Multi-Voting, Nominal Group Technique, and just picking one and going through all of them. The tool I have used the most for this, (due to its effectiveness and ease of use), is the Nominal Group Technique.

Nominal Group Technique

1. **Generating Ideas:** If a brainstorming session has been completed, the ideas generated from that session will be used for the NGT. If no brainstorming has been completed, the moderator presents the problem statement to the group in written form and reads it to the group. Each person silently generates ideas and writes them down.

2. **Recording Ideas:** Write the ideas from the team on a whiteboard, or flip chart that is visible to the entire team. Proceed until all members' ideas have been documented.

3. **Discussing Ideas:** Discuss each recorded idea to clarify and to help team members determine the relative importance of each item. This step provides an opportunity for members to express their understanding of the logic and the relative importance of the item.

4. **Voting on Ideas:** Individuals vote privately using sticky notes, to prioritize the ideas. Each team member selects the 5 most important items from the group list and writes one idea on each sticky along with their rank number for that idea, (1-5). In the case of FAPI, there were 5 potential causes

identified by the team, so the voting by the team will include all 5 potential causes.

After team members rank the responses in order of their perceived priority, the facilitator will record them on the flip chart with numbers down the right-hand side of the chart, which correspond to the ideas from the brainstorming. The ideas that are the most highly rated by the group are prioritized for the 5 Why analysis.

Nominal Group Technique – Results

Potential Cause from Brainstorming/Cause & Effect Diagram	Team Member	Team Member	Team Member	Team Member	Team Member	Totals	Ranking
	Results on voting from each team member on each potential cause						
Parts Damaged in Hobbing	2	4	3	5	4	18	4
Parts Damaged When Moved	3	3	4	2	3	15	3
Parts Damaged During Assy	4	1	2	1	2	10	2
Parts Damaged During HT	1	2	1	3	1	8	1
Parts Damaged While Loaded	5	5	5	4	5	24	5

Figure 6.7 Nominal Group Technique

In this case there were 5 potential causes identified by the team, so each team member voted to rank the potential causes from 1 to 5, with 1 being what they believe to be the most likely cause. Once all votes are tallied, the potential causes are ranked from the lowest to the highest totals. The potential cause with the lowest score is the most likely cause and is the one the team will start with when conducting the 5 Why analysis. Based on the results of the voting from the Nominal Group Technique, the team will start the 5 Why analysis with the potential cause of "parts damaged during HT".

The Source of the Problem

Now that we have determined what the problem is, (dents on gear teeth), and the team voted to prioritize "Parts Damaged While Loaded at Heat Treat", it was decided by the team to perform a process study to further validate that they should focus on the Heat Treat process. Sometimes it is helpful to understand where the problem is, or what the source of the problem is. Just like knowing what the problem is does not tell us the root cause, knowing the source also does not tell us the root cause, but it does help to narrow our focus.

Since we created a process map in a previous step, we can set up a study with a controlled group of parts and follow them through every step of the process, inspecting the gears for dents following each process step.

In looking at the Pareto diagram from the controlled study, it is obvious that the biggest issue with damaging the gear teeth is coming from the heat treat process step. We still do not know why or how to fix it, but we do know where to focus our efforts. Again, knowing the source does not tell us why the problem occurred and knowing the source should not point to who caused it or whom to blame.

It is not always easy, or even practical to do this type of study, but it worked out in this case and because of it we have more than the team's collective educated opinions and experience to tell them where to focus.

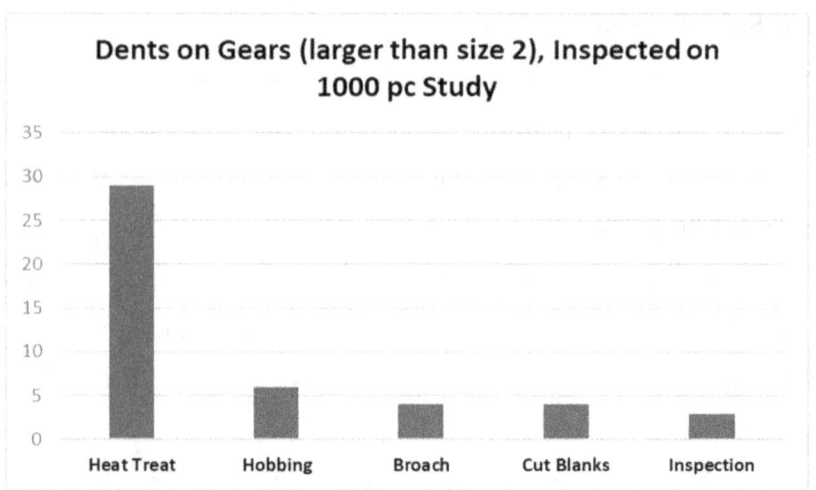

Figure 6.8 Pareto Diagram of Gear Damage

7. 5-Why Analysis

"Ask Why five times about every matter", Taiichi Ohno. (Liker, 2021). The previous quote from Toyota's Chief Engineer when asked in an interview to explain the improved quality levels achieved at Toyota. Of course, Ohno was also acknowledged as the primary architect of the Toyota Production System, (TPS), which became the modern footprint for modern Lean Manufacturing systems around the world.

What Ohno was referring to is now a widely used Root Cause Analysis tool known as the 5 Why Analysis. The tool is very useful in drilling down from a high-level symptom down to the lowest level cause, (the root cause), of a problem. When used properly, the tool demonstrates the concept that some of the biggest problems are often initially caused by much smaller issues.

The first rule for conducting a 5 Why Analysis is that there are not always exactly 5 Whys. There may be more than 5, or less than 5. Do not make the mistake of restricting your thought process by confining yourself to exactly 5 because doing so almost assures that you are either truncating the RCA process by stopping short of the true root cause, or you will be adding random nonsense to complete the 5 Whys.

The 5 Why Analysis is conducted by simply taking the problem statement and asking why in succession until it no longer makes sense to keep asking why. How do we know when it no longer makes sense to keep asking why? Some pointers include making sure the answers to the whys remain linear and making sure they at least appear to be practical. Experience with conducting 5 Why Analyses helps to make this clearer.

Earlier in this chapter we discussed three different categories of Root Causes; they are the Why Made? (Occurrence), the Why Shipped? (Detection), and Why the System Failed? (Systemic). Again, depending on the purpose for the problem-solving effort, all three categories of root causes may need to be determined and corrected. One way to ensure that all three categories are addressed and that the information in each of the three 5 Why Analyses is not over-lapping into another is by using a tool called the 3 Legged 5 Why Analysis, which is further explained below.

3 Legged 5 Why Analysis

Using all three parts of the root cause analysis is called a 3 Legged 5 Why Analysis, which can be seen in Figure 6.9. The 3 Legged 5 Why Analysis has been used by many companies and is particularly helpful when the goal is zero recurrence. Ford Motor Company, General Motors, and Chrysler have all used some variation of this approach. Honda uses two of the three legs, (why made and why not detected), in their 5P approach.

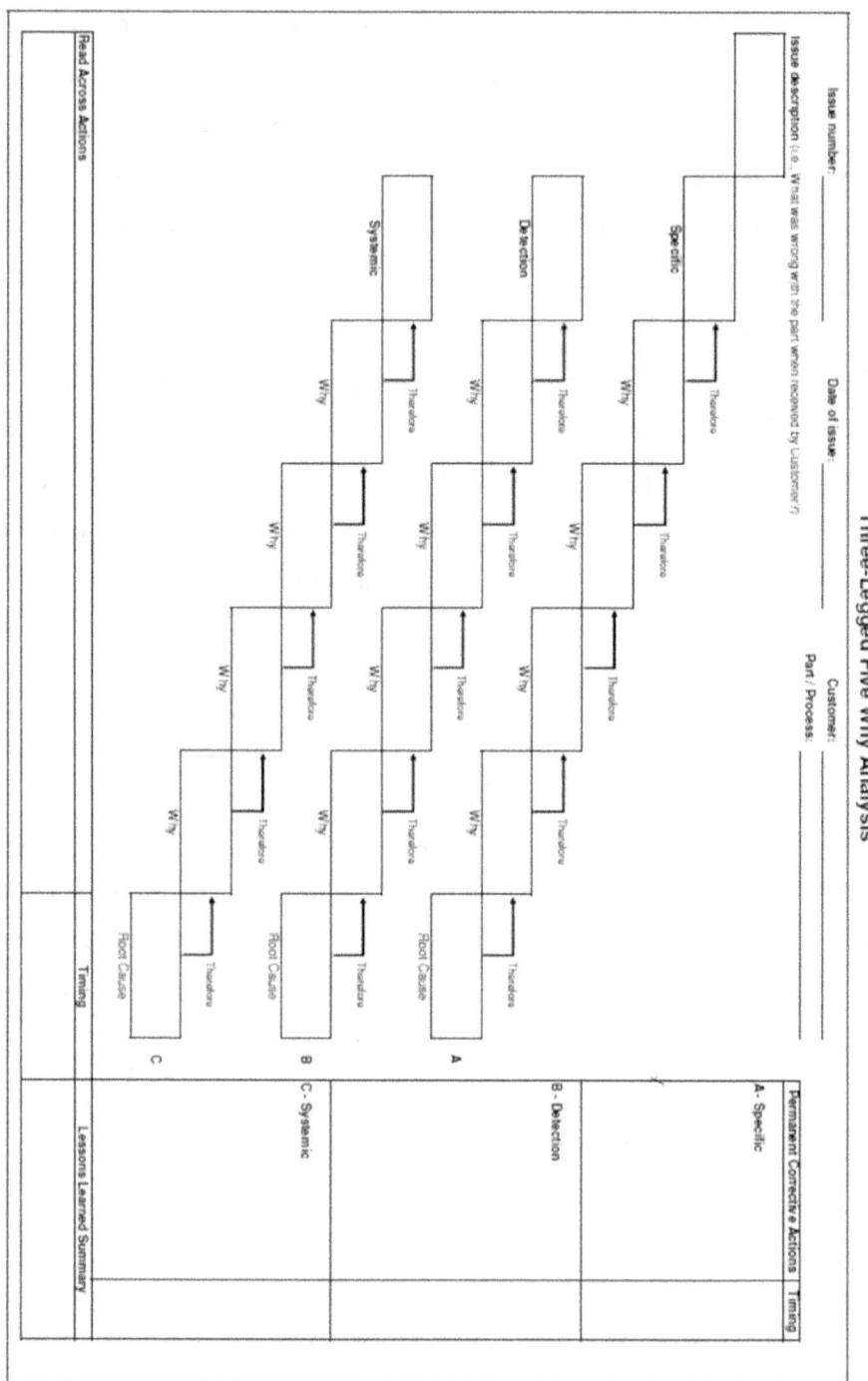

Figure 6.9 3-Legged 5 Why Analysis

Depending on the scope of the problem, all three legs of the 5 Why Analysis may need to be completed. In some cases, only two of the legs may need to be completed. For problems pertaining to the shipment of nonconforming product, *always* complete at least the Specific and the Detection legs of the root cause. I use this as a hard rule because the defect was both *made,* and it *escaped*. It is important to understand the root cause(s) for why both failures occurred, and it is crucial to ensure the root causes will not recur.

The 5 Why analysis is intended to be linear with each successive why coming from the answer to the preceding why. The next illustration, (which is a fable from Ben Franklin), is intended to help demonstrate this linearity:

The Nail and the Kingdom

For want of a nail the shoe was lost
For want of a shoe the horse was lost
For want of a horse the warrior was lost
For want of a warrior the battle was lost
For want of a battle the kingdom was lost

All for want of a nail

Figure 6.10 The Nail and the Kingdom

Steps for completing the 5 Whys Analysis
1. Take the top potential cause from the Nominal Group Technique exercise and write it at the top of the whiteboard, or flipchart.
2. Read the top line and ask the first why.
3. Write the answer below the first why and ask the second why.
4. Repeat until it is no longer logical to ask why.

One example of a 5 Why Analysis that appears to have been stopped too early is Figure 6.10 from the Nail and the Kingdom. While this example may display good linearity, it does appear to stop short of the actual root cause because it would be logical to continue to ask why at the end. "Why were there not enough nails?", etc.

Using the steps on the previous page, please review the 5 Why analysis in Figure 6.11 from the Forrester Agricultural Products, Inc. Case Study.

Forrester Agricultural Products, Inc. Case Study – 5 Why Analysis

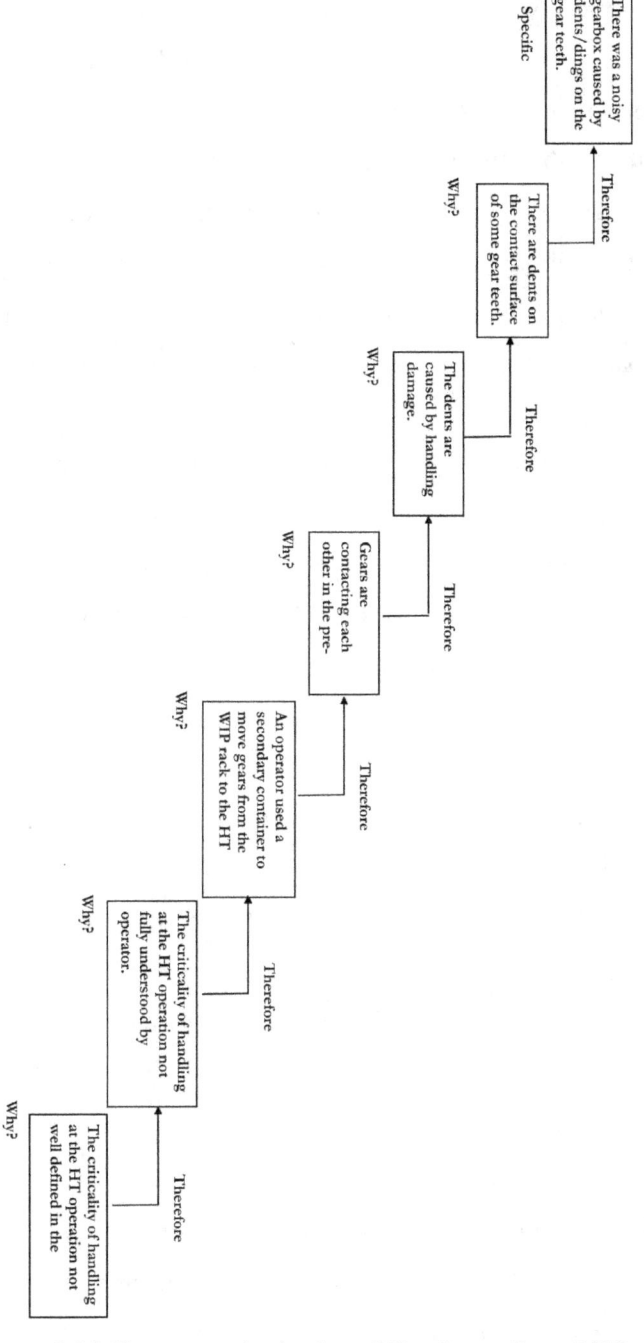

Figure 6.11 Forrester Agricultural Products, Inc. 5 Why Analysis

Review of FAPI Why Made 5 Why Analysis

Upon review of the FAPI 5 Why analysis, there are few things that we can observe. One interesting observation is that there are 6 whys and not 5. Remember to continue to ask why until it no longer makes sense to keep asking why. Another important point to note is that the main issue leading to the problem is that an operator used a secondary container to move gears from a WIP rack to load onto a HT rack. Because the criticality of safely handling the gears was not understood by the operator, they found a more efficient way to load the racks by moving multiple gears at a time using a container.

Another thing to mention about the 5 Why analysis is that the root cause pointed to an operator introducing a change point that eventually led to the defect. In some company cultures, the "root cause analysis" in this case would end with "operator error" and that would be the end of the analysis. In this case, the team kept asking why and found that the criticality of handling was not well-defined and was not understood by an inexperienced operator.

The root cause in this case is **"The use of a secondary container to move gears because the criticality of parts handling at the Heat Treat operation was not well-defined in the process".** This could be worded differently, but the main issue remains the same. Given the root cause and the fact that the defective parts were not identified in house and subsequently built into an assembled gearbox and shipped to the customer, it is likely that this was not the first such occurrence.

Make sure the Root Cause is about the Process

Another important thing to remember about conducting a root cause analysis is that the team needs to try to avoid blaming the employee when problem solving. Remember to focus the problem solving and root cause analysis on the process. In the root cause analysis above, it would have been easy to just leave it at "the operator failed to properly protect the gears from getting damaged". This kind of root cause is usually followed by a predictable corrective action like, "wrote up operator", or "retrained operator". Standalone corrective actions like retraining the operator always leads me to ask whether the operator was not trained in the first place and if they were, how will retraining them help when the first training apparently did not work? Training is an important part of implementing containment, corrective, and preventive actions, but it is not complete as a standalone corrective action and it is not likely to prevent recurrence.

This may seem redundant, but it bears repeating: if the goal is to make sure this problem does not happen again, the corrective actions typically associated with blaming the employee are not usually going to accomplish that. Instead of blaming the employee, always try to make it about the process. When the team is focused on an operator, or employee, being the root cause of a problem, always ask the following question: **"what about the process allowed the operator to err?"**

Test for linearity

As important as linearity is to properly conducting a 5 Why analysis, there is a simple test that anyone can apply in seconds to ensure linearity. The test I am referring to is called the Reverse Logic Test, (I have also heard this test referred to as the "therefore" test). The reverse logic test is a quick, simple way to check the linearity of the logic used to develop the 5 Whys analysis. Simply go to the last answer in the series of why questions and use that as the starting point and go back up the chain using statements of, therefore.

The example 5 Whys analysis and Reverse Logic test in Figure 6-12 is based on a fable from Ben Franklin. To complete the Reverse Logic test, start at the end, (or the last answer to why), and reverse the order with statements like the following: there were not enough nails, therefore a horse lost a shoe, therefore there was one less horse, therefore there was one less warrior, therefore the battle was lost, and therefore the kingdom was lost. You should be able to transition smoothly and naturally from the last to the first why in the 5 Why analysis. In this case, there is a smooth transition through all the statements back to the original statement. This example passes the linearity test. A pointer to remember is that good linearity does not necessarily mean that you have the real root cause, but it does mean that the 5 Why analysis was properly completed.

Example of Good Linearity

			Reverse Logic Test	Linear Step?
Result	Lost the Kingdom	→	Therefore	Yes
1. Why?	Lost the Battle	→	Therefore	Yes
2. Why?	One Less Warrior	→	Therefore	Yes
3. Why?	One Less Horse	→	Therefore	Yes
4. Why?	Horse Lost a Shoe	→	Therefore	Yes
5. Why?	Not Enough Nails	→	Therefore	

Figure 6.12 Good Linearity Example

Now, review the next 5 Why example in Figure 6.13 that is identified as "Bad Linearity" and apply the reverse logic test. You will notice that you cannot easily transition from the last answer to the problem and therefore the 5 why analysis is not linear.

Example of Bad Linearity

			Reverse Logic Test	Linear Step?
Result	Parts out of Spec	→	Therefore	No
1. Why?	The tool broke	→	Therefore	No
2. Why?	The operator did not properly inspect the parts	→	Therefore	No
3. Why?	The machine was crashed and not properly reset	→	Therefore	No
4. Why?	The gage was missing	→	Therefore	No
5. Why?	The operator was new and not properly trained	→	Therefore	

Figure 6.13 Bad Linearity Example

8. Return to the Process and Verify Root Cause(s)

Once the team has agreed to the most likely root cause(s) of the issue, take the following steps to verify that the root cause(s) identified lead to the condition:

1. Compare the root cause to the **Problem Statement**. Does the root cause address the problem as defined?
2. Compare the root cause to the **5W2H Not Analysis** that was completed while creating the problem statement. Does the root cause align with what was presented as known information?
3. Apply a **Reverse Logic Test** the 5 Why analysis and see if there is smooth transition from the last why answer to the initial problem at the beginning of the 5 Why Analysis. Is the 5 Why Analysis linear, or do the responses appear to be non-linear and random?
4. **Ensure that the root cause addresses *Why*** the process or system failed and not who, or what.
5. See if the team can **recreate the issue** by manipulating what you have determined to be the root cause(s). This is commonly referred to as "turning the problem on and off". **Note:** This will not be practical to do in some processes. Do not force the application of this

point if doing so will be dangerous, costly, or resource draining.

Next, we will apply the 5 rules above to the Problem Solving conducted for the FAPI case study we have been working on.

- ✓ The first step is to compare the root cause to the problem statement. The problem statement is, "On May 12, 2018, Forrester Agricultural Products, Inc. reported 1 gearbox of P/N 123-XYZ produced on May 5, 2018, with excessive noise due to dents/dings on gear teeth contact surface". The root cause that the team identified does align with why the issue from the problem statement occurred. Result: **Pass**.

- ✓ The next step is to compare the root cause to the 5W2H Analysis. Again, the root cause does match up with several key items from the 5W2H Diagram. It is important to note that this comparison will not always yield an obvious alignment. Sometimes, it can work just by the absence of an obvious *misalignment*. Result: **Pass**.

- ✓ The third step is to apply the Reverse Logic test to the 5 Whys analysis. The reverse logic test was applied and there seems to be a smooth transition back to the beginning of the 5 Why Analysis. Result: **Pass**.

- ✓ The fourth root cause test is to ensure that the root cause answers why the process failed. In this case the root cause answers why and not who, or what as a matter of final root cause. Remember, both who and what are important parts of the investigation, but the root cause analysis cannot end at either who, or what. Result: **Pass**.

- ✓ The final step to verify the root cause is to see if the issue can easily be recreated by applying the root cause to the process in a controlled manner. In this case the problem can be easily recreated by the team being present while loading the gears onto racks at the Heat Treat process. They may introduce the use of a transfer container between the WIP rack and the HT rack. In doing this, they will use a controlled set of gears that are clearly marked so they can prevent the gears from this controlled study from accidentally getting mixed into the normal process stream. As was previously pointed out, recreating the process failure is not always possible, or practical. Each situation is different, and the team will apply this only as its practical. Result: **Pass**.

Root Cause for Why Not Detected

As we previously discussed, when the nonconforming product, transaction, or service went beyond the process it was performed in, it was essentially "shipped", or sent. Whenever this happens, the Why Not Detected root cause analysis should also be completed and any relevant corrective and preventive actions determined and implemented.

What is "Why Not Detected"?

The Why Not Detected root cause category is used for understanding where, why, and how a defect got out of the process. Where did the process fail to detect the nonconformance? This is often referred to as the escape point. In some cases, there may be multiple points in the process where the nonconformance *could* have been detected, but the escape point is actually the closest point near where the nonconformance was generated that it should have been detected. Once the escape point is identified, the team can focus on **Why**. (A word of caution: if there was some concern about blaming employees for the Why Made root cause, the risk is even increased with Why Not Detected. "The Operator failed to detect the issue" is an all too common "root cause" for why not detected.)

Why did the Inspection Process Fail?

Why Not Detected? (Examples)

- Process not looking for it
- Tools/methods not in place

- Tools/methods in place, but inadequate
- Not following the control plan (Inspection)
- Not following the control plan (Reaction Plan)
- Bypassed Detection/Error Proofing
- Escaped (was detected but placed back into product flow)

Process not looking for it

In this case, there is no inspection, (either automated or manual inspection), in place to detect the defect. The control plan does not list an inspection for it, which allows the defect to go undetected.

Tools/methods not in place

In this case, the inspection is required, but the proper tools were either not deployed to the process or they are missing.

Not following the control plan

In this case, the inspection is required, and the tools were provided, but for some reason the inspections are not being completed as required.

Bypassed Detection/Error Proofing

In the case of bypassed detection/error proofing, there is some device in place intended to detect/prevent the defect, but the device has been bypassed. Who usually lets us know when our error-proofing has been bypassed? Our customer!

Escaped Containment (was detected but placed back into product flow)

This is one of the most painful scenarios for why defective product was shipped. The issue was detected and it was still shipped to the customer.

5 Why Analysis for Why Not Detected

The Problem-Solving team completed the 5 Why Analysis for Why Not Detected and as you can see in Figure 6-14, it does not follow the typical textbook example of a 5 Why Analysis. The first answer to Why actually yielded two plausible answers and the Team Leader took the team down both paths to ensure the root cause was properly assessed. In both paths it is determined that the process, (at the escape point), was not looking for the defect of dented/damaged gear teeth. The root cause for Why Not Detected is: **"The Heat Treat process inspection is not looking for the defect because gear teeth damage was not identified as a significant concern as a cause of noise."**

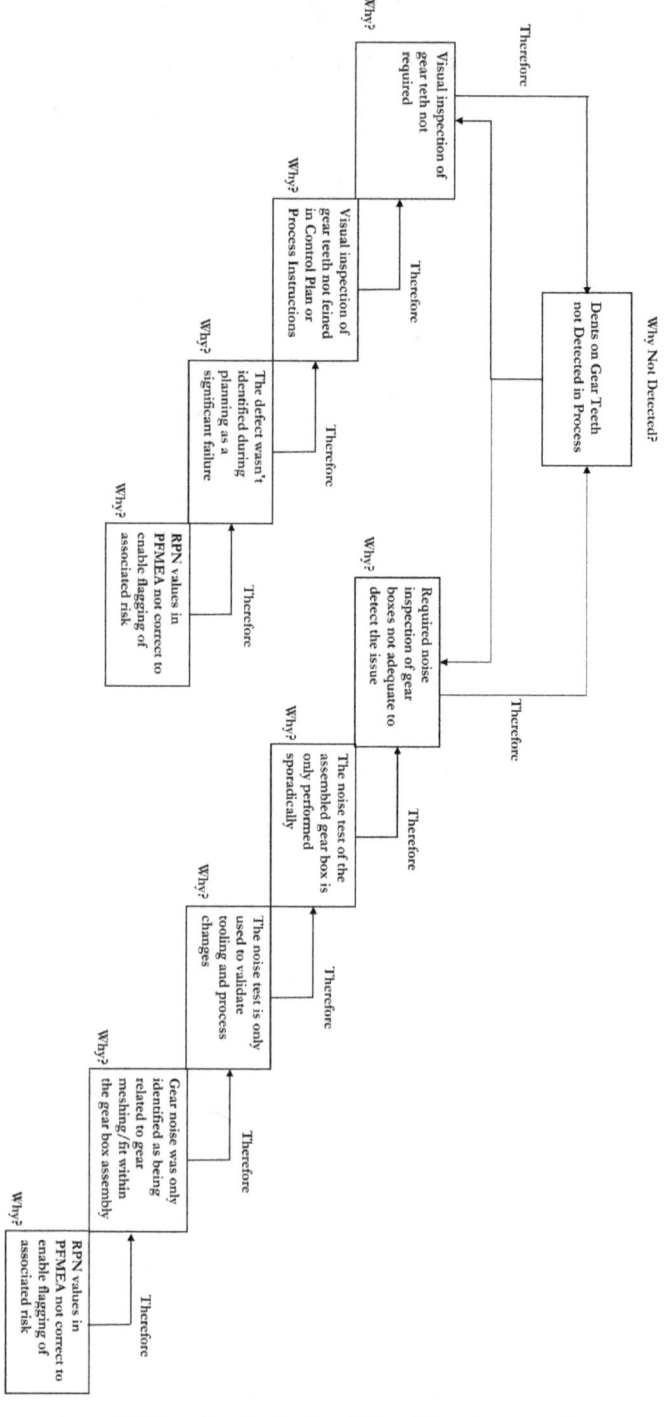

Figure 6.14 5 Why Analysis for Why Not Detected

Step 5 Pointers and Pitfalls

- Always start the Root Cause Analysis by reviewing the problem statement.

- The team should always spend some time at Gemba to get a first-hand understanding of the process.

- Use all three legs of the 5 Why analysis when necessary. In the case of shipment of nonconforming product, at a minimum do 5 Why analyses for both Why Made and Why Shipped.

- Always use the reverse logic test to check the 5 Why analysis for linearity.

Documenting Step 5 within the 8 Step format

Problem No	Source		Line	Product Family	Part Number
051218-01	Customer – Irish Poultry Products, Inc.			Gear Box/Spur Gears	123-XYZ
	Customer reference		Qty	Date & Shift Occurred	Operation #
	N/A		1 pc	5/5/18 1st shift	Gear Mfg.

Step 2 Team Members (initials/name)	Role	
T. Forrester	Champion	
F. Noe	Leader	
J. Russell	Scribe	
H. Wheatley	Timekeeper	
D. Pickerell	Team Member	
C. Morris	Process Owner	

Step 3 Description of problem

On May 12, 2018, Irish Poultry Products, Inc. reported 1 gearbox of P/N 123-XYZ produced on May 5, 2018, with excessive noise due to dents/dings on gear teeth contact surface.

Step 4 Interim Containment actions	Assigned to	Effective Date
See attached Action Plan		

Step 5 Define the root cause

Why Made? The use of a secondary container to move gears because the criticality of parts handling at the Heat Treat operation was not well-defined in the process.

Why not Detected? The Heat Treat process inspection is not looking for the defect because gear teeth damage wasn't identified as a significant concern as a cause of noise.

Step 6 Permanent Corrective Actions - Implementation, and Validation

Step 7 Preventive Actions - Implementation and Verification

Step 8 Celebrate Team Success!

Checklist	Date	Update	Date
Problem Validated?		DFMEA/PFMEA	
Containment Worksheet Completed?		Control plan(s)	
FMEA Reviewed?		Feed Across/Feed Forward	
Team includes operator?		Procedures/WI Updated	
8 Step Approved by CART?		Process Audits Implemented	
8 Step Reviewed with and presented to customer?		Training Completed	

Figure 6.15 Step 5 8-Step Report

Chapter 7

Step 6: Permanent Corrective Action Selection, Implementation, and Validation

One mistake that an experienced problem solver will recognize is when people refer to Root Cause Analysis and Problem Solving synonymously. While the terms are clearly related, they are not synonymous as evidenced by the recognition that during a root cause analysis, no action has been taken to eliminate the problem by correcting or improving anything. To gauge an applicant's understanding of Problem-Solving during interviews I will ask a candidate, "What is your favorite, or go-to Problem-Solving approach or methodology?" I often get a response like, "I do 5 Why Analysis", Or "I like Brainstorming and Fishbone Diagrams". I do too, but those are not Problem-Solving approaches per se', they are root cause analysis tools. Understanding and defining the root cause of a problem is a critical step in Problem Solving, but the job is not finished yet.

While getting to the root cause of a problem is a crucial and rewarding milestone in the Problem-Solving process, just knowing the root cause does not solve the problem. Specific actions must be taken to reduce or eliminate the root cause from occurring.

Once the Root Cause has been determined by and verified by the team, the team must define the approach to select the proper corrective action(s) and they must determine how to implement and validate the selected corrective actions. The team must determine what actions to take to permanently eliminate the root cause from occurring, thus stopping the problems/symptoms from recurring.

Corrective Action Selection

Before getting too far down the path of selecting and implementing corrective actions, there are a few important things to keep in mind:

1. The team will likely not have an open checkbook to pay for solutions. There are always cost/payback considerations to balance, even when solving a problem. The key is to find a solution that will work and that will be cost effective at the same time. Anticipate being challenged on this.

2. Make sure you are not solving one problem and causing several more. It is irresponsible to only focus on the problem at hand without considering the potential impact elsewhere. If fixing something also causes a new safety problem, or an environmental, or a quality, or other problem, then it should not be accepted as a solution. I am always shocked and left scratching my head when I hear any high-level leader question why they need to concern themselves with

things other than the scope of the problem they are solving. Think of this as a balanced scorecard where all aspects of the business must be considered. **Do not let today's solutions become or cause tomorrow's problems.**

Simple Corrective Action Selection Method – PICK Chart

Step 1: Write both the Problem Statement and the Root Cause on the whiteboard, or flipchart and review with the team. This is an important step to keep the team focused and to ensure the alignment of the proposed corrective actions to the root cause(s) of the problem.

Step 2: After reviewing the Problem Statement and the Root Cause of the problem, the team should conduct a brainstorming exercise to generate ideas to fix the root cause. This brainstorming activity must be focused on actions to correct the root cause. Once the ideas have been generated using the brainstorming process, do a sanity check to eliminate the far-fetched, non-sensical ideas and focus on the practical ideas that remain.

Step 3: Use a prioritization tool to prioritize the improvement actions that the team identified. There are many prioritization methods that can be used including the PICK chart, various prioritization matrices, and too many other techniques to mention all of them. The key is to use a method you are comfortable with and with which you have had good results in the past. If you are not sure what prioritization technique to apply, a PICK chart is simple and does not require extensive prior experience to use. For this example, we will use the PICK chart.

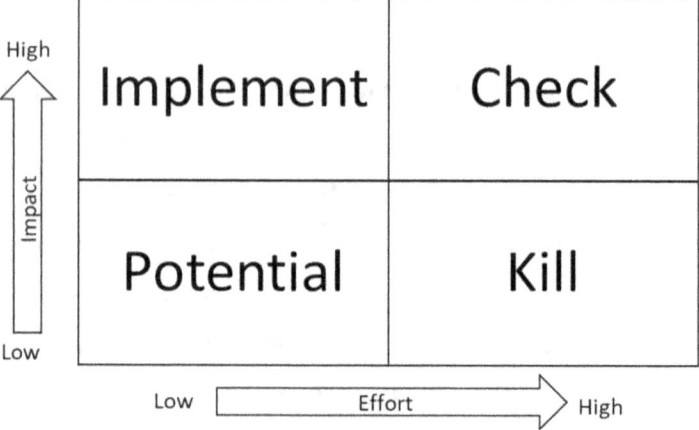

Figure 7.1 Example PICK Chart

The Meaning of PICK

Potential includes the ideas that are easy to implement but have a low expected impact.

Implement for projects that are easy to implement, with a high potential impact.

Check, which includes projects that may have a high impact, but require a high effort. Some further investigation may need to be done to determine whether to pursue.

Kill eliminates ideas that are hard to implement and with a low return.

PICK Chart Instructions

1. On a flip chart or dry erase board, draw your quad chart and label the horizontal line "Effort" and the vertical line "Impact."
2. Write each unique item on individual sticky notes.
3. Rank the items from least (left) to most (right) effort.
    a. Place the sticky note with the lowest ranked effort on the left end of the center line of the matrix and arrange the rest of the sticky notes in order across the same line from low to high, (from left to right).
4. Keeping your sticky notes in the order of their effort rankings,

move them up (high) or down (low) based on their relative impact.

5. (Note: If the team does not have a good understanding of the approximate Impact/Effort of solutions, they will need to consult with the Champion, or other sources of knowledge).

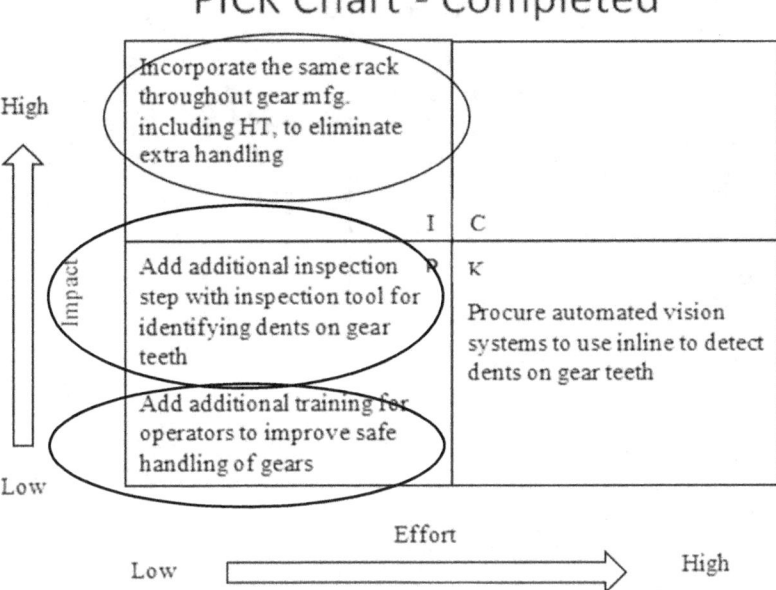

Figure 7.2 Completed PICK Chart for Corrective Actions

Step 4: Review the final list of improvement actions with the Problem-Solving champion. At this point, the champion will act as a sounding board to ensure the actions seem feasible and that the resources are available to implement and maintain the improvements.

Step 5: Create a detailed action plan based on the prioritized list of corrective actions. The action plan must include what actions are planned, who is responsible for the action, and when it is planned to be completed.

Step 6: The Problem-Solving team leader must continue to conduct team meetings to track the completion of the corrective actions as well as the results of validation activities. The team leader and team members should determine the meeting frequency based on the timing of planned activities.

No.	Action Item	C	CA	PA	Owner	Due	Actual
1.	Determine number of racks needed		X		WR	5/30/18	5/26/18
2.	Complete the design work to ensure the racks will work in all processes including Heat Treat		X		MM	6/11/18	6/12/18
3.	Outsource production of prototype rack to trial in process		X		FR	6/12/18	6/14/18
4.	Run trial through production processes using prototype rack		X		WR	7/13/18	7/15/18
5.	Outside source to complete build of all racks needed		X		PVW	9/10/18	9/08/18
6.	Complete work instructions to define proper use of new racks		X		PVW	8/3/18	8/13/18
7.	Feed Across corrective actions to the other production lines		X		WR	7/25/18	9/24/18
8.	Train affected employees in CAs		X		WR	9/13/18	9/13/18
C = Containment, CA = Corrective Action, PA = Preventive Action							

Figure 7.3 Permanent Corrective Action – Action Plan

Validation

Validate the effectiveness of the corrective actions by applying a trend chart to the process affected by the corrective actions. It is important that the team selects an appropriate KPI, (or KPIs), to measure the *effectiveness* of the corrective actions. ISO-9000:2015 defines effectiveness as the "extent to which planned activities are realized and planned results achieved", (International Standard ISO-9000:2015). The KPI being tracked and evaluated should be consistent throughout the Problem-Solving process and should be aligned with KPIs tracked through Lean Daily Management, or Tier Meetings, if applicable. This will allow the team to demonstrate the before and after improvement and tracking it will help to alert the process owners when a change has occurred.

In addition to tracking the process KPIs, other important methods to employ during the corrective action validation phase include process audits, process reviews, and corrective action reviews through the use of a Problem-Solving Review Team, (see chapter 11).

Pareto charts are used for a variety of data collection and analysis. They are especially useful in the quantification of problems and they can be very useful in providing some validation that implemented actions have had the intended impact on improving the output from the process. Pareto diagrams can provide a simple comparative analysis and are based on an observation by its creator, Wilfredo Pareto who observed that 80% of the problems were from 20% of the categories, (this is the basis for the 80/20 rule).

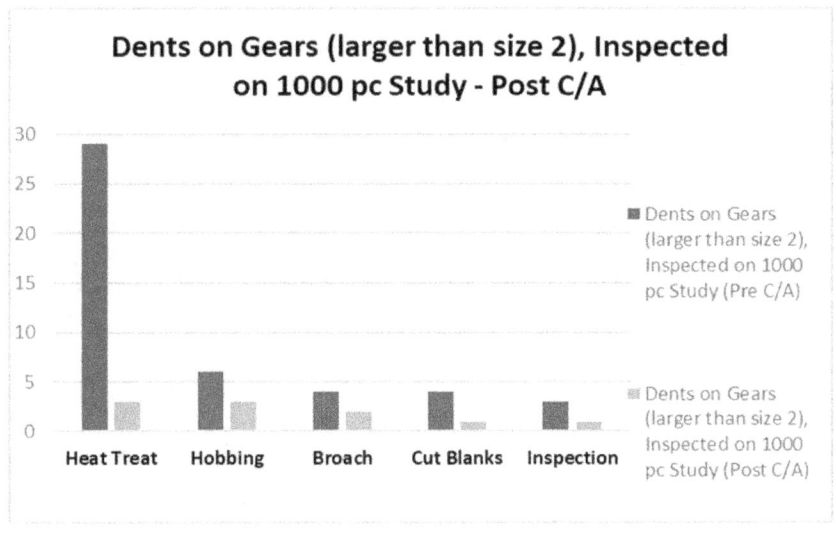

Figure 7.4 Pareto Chart – Post C/A (Validation)

Step 6 Pointers and Pitfalls

- Make sure the team spends an adequate amount of time analyzing options for corrective actions. Do not jump to pre-conceived ideas about this.

- Use a PICK chart or other method for evaluating potential corrective actions.

- Do data analysis to validate the effectiveness of the corrective actions by monitoring process results through trend charts, Pareto Diagrams, or other methods.

Documenting Step 6 within the 8 Step format

Problem No	Source		Line	Product Family	Part Number
051218-01	Customer – Irish Poultry Products, Inc.			Gear Box/Spur Gears	123-XYZ
	Customer reference		Qty	Date & Shift Occurred	Operation #
	N/A		1 pc	5/5/18 1st shift	Gear Mfg.

Step 2 Team Members (initials/name)	Role
T. Forrester	Champion
F. Noe	Leader
J. Russell	Scribe
H. Wheatley	Timekeeper
D. Pickerell	Team Member
C. Morris	Process Owner

Step 3 Description of problem

On May 12, 2018, Irish Poultry Products, Inc. reported 1 gearbox of P/N 123-XYZ produced on May 5, 2018, with excessive noise due to dents/dings on gear teeth contact surface.

Step 4 Interim Containment actions	Assigned to	Effective Date
See attached Action Plan		

Step 5 Define the root cause

Why Made? The use of a secondary container to move gears because the criticality of parts handling at the Heat Treat operation was not well-defined in the process.

Why not Detected? The Heat Treat process inspection is not looking for the defect because gear teeth damage wasn't identified as a significant concern as a cause of noise.

Step 6 Permanent Corrective Actions - Implementation, and Validation

See attached action plan

Step 7 Preventive Actions - Implementation and Verification

Step 8 Celebrate Team Success!

Checklist	Date	Update	Date
Problem Validated?		DFMEA/PFMEA	
Containment Worksheet Completed?		Control plan(s)	
FMEA Reviewed?		Feed Across/Feed Forward	
Team includes operator?		Procedures/WI Updated	
8 Step Approved by CART?		Process Audits Implemented	
8 Step Reviewed with and presented to customer?		Training Completed	

Figure 7.5 Step 6 8-Step Report

Chapter 8

Step 7: Preventive Actions Implementation and Verification

Preventive Actions

The definition for Preventive Action provided by ASQ is, "Action taken to prevent occurrence of nonconformances", (ASQ, 2021). The definition provided by ISO-9000 standard is, "action to eliminate the cause of a potential *nonconformity* or other potential undesirable situation", (International Standard ISO-9000:2015). It is important to note that the difference between corrective and preventive action is that corrective action is taken to prevent something that has happened from happening again or recurring whereas preventive actions are taken to prevent something from happening that either has not occurred yet, or to prevent something that has occurred somewhere from occurring in another location, process, cell, machine, etc. These simple definitions are explicit in stating that preventive actions are all about taking some planned action to prevent the occurrence of the cause of nonconformance.

Preventing recurrence generally follows two primary themes:

1. *Institutionalizing* the improvements that were made as corrective actions.
2. Sustaining the gains that were made as corrective actions.

Institutionalizing improvements includes all the things required to make those improvements *a way of life*. When we think about preventing recurrence, we should always think in terms of preventing the same cause from recurring as well as preventing it from happening to another product, within another process, or at another location.

Some of the tools typically used for preventive actions include the following and we will look at how these tools are used as preventive actions: Control Plans, Mistake Proofing, Feed Across/Feed Forward, FMEA, Layered Process Audits, Lessons Learned, Trend Charts, and Training. For a step-by-step process to employ for identifying the proper and necessary preventive actions, please see the steps below:

Steps to Determining Preventive Actions

1. Review the Problem Statement and Corrective Actions with the team.
2. Brainstorm a list of possible Preventive Actions.
3. Review as a team and determine which are applicable.
4. Apply Feed Across/Feed Forward methodology.

Update all related systems documentation, including the following at a minimum:

- ✓ FMEA
- ✓ Control Plan
- ✓ Procedures/Work Instructions
- ✓ Design Records
- ✓ ERP information such as Bills of Materials (as applicable)
- ✓ Train all applicable associates in the changes stemming from the preventive actions.
- ✓ Establish/update process audits to ensure continued implementation and effectiveness of corrective and preventive actions.
- ✓ Update the Problem-Solving record to include the preventive actions.

Update the Control Plan

Control plans are road maps for how key product, or service features are controlled through controlling the process that generates those features. Corrective Actions that are made by changing any aspect of the process should be captured by updating the control plan. As we look at the example in Figure 8.1, any changes to specifications, inspection methods or frequencies, process sequence, etc. are documented within the control plan. In this case, inspections are added as part of the corrective actions made in response to the Why Not Detected root cause.

CONTROL PLAN

☐ Prototype ☐ Pre-Launch ☑ Production

Control Plan Number		Key Contact/Phone		Date (Orig.)	Date (Rev.)
		Tracy Forrester		2/18/2016	7/22/2018
Part Number/Latest Change Level		Core Team		Customer Engineering Approval/Date (If Req'd.)	
123/XYZ				N/A	
Part Name/Description		Supplier/Plant Approval/Date		Customer Quality Approval/Date (If Req'd.)	
Spur Gear				N/A	

PART/ PROCESS NUMBER	PROCESS NAME/ OPERATION DESCRIPTION	MACHINE, DEVICE JIG, TOOLS FOR MFG.	CHARACTERISTICS		SPECIAL CHAR. CLASS	PRODUCT/PROCESS SPECIFICATION/ TOLERANCE	METHODS				REACTION PLAN
			NO.	PRODUCT/ PROCESS			EVALUATION/ MEASUREMENT TECHNIQUE	SAMPLE SIZE	SAMPLE FREQ.	RESPONSIBLE FOR MEAS.	CONTROL METHOD
Spur Gears	Internal Spline	N/A	17	Gear Teeth Dents	N/A	No dents on gear contact surface larger than size 2	Visual	3 Pcs	Per Hr	Operator	Document on Check Sheet	Quarantine suspect/defective gears Contact Team Leader
	Hobbing						Mylar Dent Size Chart	1	As needed	Operator	Document on Check Sheet	Quarantine suspect/defective gears Contact Team Leader
	Inspection											
	Heat Treat											

Figure 8.1 Control Plan

Update the FMEA

The applicable FMEA should be updated during every Problem-Solving effort. The example in Figure 8.2 is from the customer concern from the FAPI case study. Whenever the FMEA is updated due to a problem and the resulting improvements to the process, I always recommend that the issue and improvements be added to the "Recommended Actions" area on the right-hand side of the FMEA form. Once added, I always recommend that the notes be kept in place going forward. I have previously seen examples of the updates being made within the original sections on the left-hand side of the FMEA form and I always have to look at the revision log just to see what was updated in the FMEA. The preference is to have the history of problems and improvements clearly visible.

Another thought to share regarding the FMEA updates is that the majority of actions that can be taken to improve the process will not result in a reduction in the Severity ranking of the FMEA. The Severity ranking will only be reduced through significant design change. The majority of FMEA Risk reduction comes from reducing the likelihood of the issues occurring, (Occurrence), or by increasing the likelihood of detecting the issues if it does occur, (Detection). The actions taken in the example below brought improvements to both the Occurrence and Detection factors, resulting in a significant reduction in the overall RPN, but there was no change to the Severity of the issue.

SEV	OCC	DET	RPN	Action Recommended	Action Taken	SEV	OCC	DET	RPN
7	4	5	140	5/12/18 - Forrester Agricultural Products, Inc. had 1 gearbox with noisy gears 1. Implement common racks to be used throught the process to reduce need for gear handling 2. Add inspection method to increase the ability to detect damaged gear teeth	1. Implemented common racks to be used throught the process to reduce need for gear handling 2. Added inspection method to increase the ability to detect damaged gear teeth	7	2	3	42

Figure 8.2 Updated FMEA

Feed Across/Feed Forward

Feed Across/Feed Forward is one of the most important preventive actions to consider. This tool, in part, comes from a Japanese method called yokoten. Yokoten is defined as "a Japanese term that loosely translates into "horizontal deployment." Yokoten is the act of sharing improvements, lessons learned and insights across the organization. Not only are the results and benefits shared but also the process that led to the result, allowing others to copy and adapt", (Gemba Academy, 2021). Even though the Feed Across/Feed Forward approach is employed following the discovery of a problem, it is also a critical proactive measure to ensure that the same issue does not occur beyond the original incident. Feed Across/Feed Forward is a tool used at the following opportunities to apply the containment, corrective, and preventive actions to ensure the same or similar issue does not occur elsewhere:

1. Additional customer locations (External)
2. Additional supplier locations (External)
3. Additional business locations (Internal)
4. Additional departments (Internal)
5. Additional processes (Internal)
6. Additional products or services (Internal)

As is evident from the list above, the opportunities are divided between external opportunities and internal opportunities. Just as it sounds, the external opportunities involve those items that are external to the organization, (like additional customer and supplier locations). The internal opportunities include those items that are internal to the organization like, additional departments, processes, and product, or services.

The tool itself is a simple matrix, an example of which is included in Figure 8.3. It starts with entering some basic information about the original occurrence of the problem. On the Y axis it lists the root cause, containment actions taken, and preventive and corrective actions taken. On the X axis it lists the various opportunities to be reviewed. The matrix itself is populated with "O" for the original occurrence, and an "A" for applicable opportunities. Once populated, the team must consider appropriate actions for those opportunities identified as applicable.

Going through this exercise can help prevent an issue from happening on another part, at another process, in another department, location, or supplier or customer location. Failure to do this can lead to multiple issues in multiple locations that could have been prevented. Some customers I have worked with in the past have required this activity along with notification to all customer locations that I shipped a product to once an issue was discovered to affect one location. In turn, I successfully applied the same approach to my own supply base.

From the example included, we can see that the team found that the problem and actions could be applicable to additional part numbers and additional machine processes, but not to additional departments, locations, suppliers, or customer locations.

Forrester Agricultural Products, Inc. - Feed Across/Feed Forward

Origin of Issue		
Date of Issue:	12-May-18	
Customer:	Irish Poultry Products	
Internal Dept:	Gear Manufacturing	
Part #:	1213-XYZ	
Problem Statement	On May 12, 2018, Irish Poultry Products, Inc. reported 1 gearbox of P/N 123-XYZ produced on May 5, 2018, with excessive noise due to dents/dings on gear teeth contact surface	
Defect:	Dents on Gear Teeth	

		Root Cause(s): Gear Mfg process not adequately defined	Containment Action(s): Sort all product visually and with mylar defect template	Corrective/Preventive Action(s): Design common gear racks to reduce handling damage
Feed Forward	Lessons Learned Database	A	A	
	Process Design Stds for Safe Gear Handling	A	A	
	Risk Analysis Std for FMEA Development	A		
External	Customer Loc 1 (Original)		O	
	Customer Loc 2			
	Supplier Loc 1			
	Supplier Loc 2			
Feed Across — Internal	Internal Ship/Dept/Function 1	O	O	O
	Internal Ship/Dept/Function 2			
	Internal Ship/Dept/Function 3			
	Machine/Process 1	A	A	A
	Machine/Process 2	A	A	A
	Machine/Process 3	O	O	O
	Machine/Process 4	A	A	A
	Machine/Process 5	A	A	A
	Part/Project No: 1 (123-XYZ)	O	O	O
	Part/Project No: 2	A	A	A
	Part/Project No: 3	A	A	A

O = Original Process for the issue, containment, or corrective/preventive actions. A = Applicable Process for the issue, containment, or corrective/preventive actions

Figure 8.3 Feed Forward/Feed Across Matrix

Step 7: Pointers and Pitfalls

- Institutionalizing improvements includes all the things required to make those improvements *a way of life*.

- Always update the FMEA during every Problem-Solving effort. Make sure to include both the incident and the resulting RPN changes from the improvements implemented.

- When applicable, make sure the control plan, instructions, designs, BOMs, programs, etc. are updated.

- Always look for opportunities to Feed Across/Feed Forward any improvements made.

Documenting Step 7 within the 8 Step format

Problem No	Source		Line	Product Family	Part Number
051218-01	Customer – Irish Poultry Products, Inc.			Gear Box/Spur Gears	123-XYZ
	Customer reference		Qty	Date & Shift Occurred	Operation #
	N/A		1 pc	5/5/18 1st shift	Gear Mfg.

Step 2 Team Members (initials/name)	Role
T. Forrester	Champion
F. Noe	Leader
J. Russell	Scribe
H. Wheatley	Timekeeper
D. Pickerell	Team Member
C. Morris	Process Owner

Step 3 Description of problem
On May 12, 2018, Irish Poultry Products, Inc. reported 1 gearbox of P/N 123-XYZ produced on May 5, 2018, with excessive noise due to dents/dings on gear teeth contact surface.

Step 4 Interim Containment actions	Assigned to	Effective Date
See attached Action Plan		

Step 5 Define the root cause
Why Made? The use of a secondary container to move gears because the criticality of parts handling at the Heat Treat operation was not well-defined in the process.
Why not Detected? The Heat Treat process inspection is not looking for the defect because gear teeth damage wasn't identified as a significant concern as a cause of noise.

Step 6 Permanent Corrective Actions - Implementation, and Validation

See attached action plan

Step 7 Preventive Actions - Implementation and Verification

See attached action plan

Step 8 Celebrate Team Success!

Checklist		Date	Update		Date
Problem Validated?	✓	5/12/18	DFMEA/PFMEA	✓	9/12/18
Containment Worksheet Completed?	✓	5/12/18	Control plan(s)	✓	7/14/18
FMEA Reviewed?	✓	5/16/18	Feed Across/Feed Forward	✓	9/24/18
Team includes operator?		5/14/19	Procedures/WI Updated	✓	8/13/18
8 Step Approved by CART?		TBD	Process Audits Implemented	✓	9/17/18
8 Step Reviewed with and presented to customer?	✓	6/19/18	Training Completed	✓	9/13/18

Figure 8.4 Step 7 8-Step Report

Chapter 9

Step 8: Celebrate Team Success!

The last formal step in the Problem-Solving process is also one of the most ignored. When I say it is ignored, I do not mean that it is only given some cursory consideration or is glossed over, I mean it is often completely ignored. Many companies who employ a similarly structured Problem-Solving process completely leave this step out of it. Some companies have a 7-step process, a 6-step process, or a 5-step process and they are all similar in that they have most of the common elements of the Problem-Solving process and they are all similar in that they leave this step out.

There are various reasons for some organizations to not include formal focus on this including that they believe employee recognition is such an integral part of their culture there is no need to call it out separately. There are always different ways to approach things, but my preference is to be intentional and focused about employee recognition.

There are many reasons for and benefits to recognizing involvement in Problem Solving. Formal recognition of Problem-Solving participation is a great way to create buy-in of the Problem-Solving process. It also helps to ensure the participants will help in the future by joining another team. The importance of recognition when it comes to building a strong Problem-Solving culture also cannot be under stated. Employees seeing other employees being recognized and employees talking with other employees about being recognized can help to gain excitement about the process.

So, what does recognition look like? There are many approaches to employee recognition. For starters, once a team has successfully completed the Problem-Solving process, they should be invited to provide a report-out presentation to the leadership team. This is a simple way to show leadership support for the process and to provide an opportunity for the team members to get some visibility with the leadership team. This can be a highly effective way to help employees to feel valued and empowered.

Other simple methods to recognize Problem-Solving team members for their involvement and contributions to successfully solving problems include presenting them with a certificate of appreciation, coffee mugs with the company logo, a company paid lunch, t-shirts with the company logo, etc. The point is that successful recognition does not have to cost much or be disruptive to the organization. Whatever the cost is, the valuable impact on morale and culture will far outweigh the less than $20 cost for each of the items I mentioned.

The cost of not doing something simple and inexpensive to recognize employees for their contributions to a successful Problem-Solving team can have a negative impact on the organization. Just as positive recognition can positively impact the morale and culture, doing nothing to provide recognition will also be talked about and remembered by employees participating on teams.

Step 8: Pointers and Pitfalls

- This step is crucial for helping to build trust and a culture of Problem Solving.
- The Team Leader needs to collaborate with the Champion to ensure that this step is not overlooked.
- The more that Senior Leadership and the peers of the team are involved in this, the more rewarding it is for the team members.
- Applicable recognition can be kept simple and may include a visible presentation of the activities and results of the team's efforts, an inexpensive lunch, a certificate, etc.
- The only way to fail at this step is to do nothing, which is done far too often.

Documenting Step 8 within the 8 Step format

Problem No	Source		Line	Product Family	Part Number
051218-01	Customer – Irish Poultry Products, Inc.			Gear Box/Spur Gears	123-XYZ
	Customer reference		Qty	Date & Shift Occurred	Operation #
	N/A		1 pc	5/5/18 1st shift	Gear Mfg.

Step 2 Team Members (initials/name)	Role
T. Forrester	Champion
F. Noe	Leader
J. Russell	Scribe
H. Wheatley	Timekeeper
D. Pickerell	Team Member
C. Morris	Process Owner

Step 3 Description of problem

On May 12, 2018, Irish Poultry Products, Inc. reported 1 gearbox of P/N 123-XYZ produced on May 5, 2018, with excessive noise due to dents/dings on gear teeth contact surface.

Step 4 Interim Containment actions	Assigned to	Effective Date
See attached Action Plan		

Step 5 Define the root cause

Why Made? The use of a secondary container to move gears because the criticality of parts handling at the Heat Treat operation was not well-defined in the process.

Why not Detected? The Heat Treat process inspection is not looking for the defect because gear teeth damage wasn't identified as a significant concern as a cause of noise.

Step 6 Permanent Corrective Actions - Implementation, and Validation

See attached action plan

Step 7 Preventive Actions - Implementation and Verification

See attached action plan

Step 8 Celebrate Team Success!

The team presented the 8 Step Problem-Solving efforts and results to Sr. management and were recognized for their contributions with lunch and certificates of achievement.

Checklist		Date	Update		Date
Problem Validated?	✓	5/12/18	DFMEA/PFMEA	✓	9/12/18
Containment Worksheet Completed?	✓	5/12/18	Control plan(s)	✓	7/14/18
FMEA Reviewed?	✓	5/16/18	Feed Across/Feed Forward	✓	9/24/18
Team includes operator?	✓	5/14/19	Procedures/WI Updated	✓	8/13/18
8 Step Approved by CART?		TBD	Process Audits Implemented	✓	9/17/18
8 Step Reviewed with and presented to customer?	✓	6/19/18	Training Completed	✓	9/13/18

Figure 8.1 Step 8 8-Step Report

Chapter 10

Establishing a Culture for Problem Solving

The entire book, to this point, has been a detailed presentation of a structured Problem-Solving process and the tools required to make it work effectively. The book goes into some details and nuances of following the structured approach described and utilizing the tools required to successfully navigate through each of the various steps within the process. It is intended as a how-to for correcting and preventing certain types of problems.

Many companies in various industries have been very successful in applying this process, but the degree of success that other organizations achieve can vary greatly depending on many variables, one of which is the culture of the organization or division.

When talking about the culture of an organization we are really talking about the beliefs and values that are not only talked about and espoused, but which are presented in the form of behaviors. These behaviors become institutionalized through clearly communicated and reinforced expectations. We are talking about a way of life. Leaders in organizations need to incorporate formal Problem Solving into the culture of their processes, departments, branches, business units, locations, divisions, organizations, etc.

As is the case with many other initiatives, approaches, and methods, if the culture to promote, encourage, convince, demand, and reinforce the employment of a structured approach to solving problems does not exist, the results can suffer and the long-term impacts on the business can be disastrous. Throughout this chapter we will look at and address various approaches to building a positive culture as it relates to real Problem Solving and truly correcting and preventing the recurrence of costly problems.

Accountability

When people discuss accountability as it relates to Quality in an organization, it is often met with negative thoughts and feelings. People often associate accountability with some type of punishment, or discipline. This association of accountability to punishment can make it difficult to have productive conversations about building a culture of accountability.

In his book titled *Winning with Accountability*, Henry J. Evans, (Evans 8), says the following about a culture of accountability: "A Culture of Accountability makes a good organization great and a great organization unstoppable". Evans further goes on define accountability as "Clear commitments that – in the eyes of others – have been kept", (Evans, 10). Based on this definition, accountability is more about keeping commitments and expecting that commitments are met versus some type of punishment.

Another aspect of accountability that may be over-looked, but is critical nonetheless, is the concept of **collective accountability**. Collective accountability is the idea that the whole is greater than the sum of its parts. It is the idea that one person cannot truly succeed when the team fails. It may mean that having a running back on a football team run for 150 yards and 3 touchdowns, (while the team lost), may have been less important than helping a teammate block the all-American linebacker on the other team on some plays. In the workplace it may mean that pointing to your success of meeting your deadline while the project failed, is not an acceptable behavior and your individual accomplishment may have been less important than seeing what you could have done to help the rest of the team succeed.

In practice, collective accountability is a willingness to challenge others in a non-threatening way to ensure commitments are kept. Conversely, it is also the willingness to be challenged by others in a non-threatening way. If collective accountability is properly applied, the growth of a culture can be significant.

Another aspect of accountability is stopping the practice of rewarding behavior that is counter-productive to what you are trying to accomplish organizationally. This can be more difficult than it sounds as this will sometimes include correcting behaviors that were previously accepted, or even rewarded. One example of this may include stopping the practice of rewarding the firefighting behavior of looking for quick fixes. Quick fixes are often counter-productive to having the discipline to put the work in to employing a structured approach to permanently solving problems. Cultures that reward firefighting often unwittingly find themselves **rewarding the arsonists for putting out the fires they started.**

Learning and Reinforcing the Language of Problem Solving

Part of establishing and reinforcing a culture of Problem Solving is paying attention to and reinforcing the language of Problem Solving. The language of Problem Solving includes the words and phrases that are said by leaders and team members when there is a problem to be solved. When describing a language of Problem Solving, the differences in language between a Problem-Solving culture and a recurring problem culture may seem subtle and insignificant, but the more ingrained Problem Solving becomes in a culture, the more obvious these differences become.

The language of Problem Solving is not a formal culture with slogans, posters, assessments, and surveys. It is often more informal and nuanced than it is obvious. The language can be heard during meetings, in various conversations, and is seen in emails and reports. The language of a recurring problem culture is common and can become so normal and so deeply ingrained in the culture of an organization that it is imperceptible to anyone but those who are well-versed in a Problem-Solving language. A comment like, "I can solve the problem because I've solved it several times before", is accepted and often rewarded by well-intending leaders who are not fluent in the language of Problem Solving.

What is the point in discussing the way people talk about Problem Solving? The point is simply to be able to pick up on key words and phrases that are used to describe Problem-Solving activities so we can identify where a culture is relative to Problem Solving. Once that is understood, training and reinforcement can be used to start changing the culture to one that not only accepts a structured approach to Problem Solving, but one that expects it.

It should be obvious that solving a problem permanently the first time and preventing it from recurring, or occurring elsewhere in the organization, is far less costly and far more impactful on increased customer satisfaction than having recurring problems. One of the aspects of getting there is to create and reinforce the right culture for Problem Solving and one of the keys to that is paying attention to the language of Problem Solving.

The table in Figure 10.1 lists several items that will often be stated differently in organizations that have a mature Problem-Solving culture and organizations that do not. Again, this may seem subtle, but when leaders and other team members can identify and are willing to apply collective accountability to the right language and behaviors, the culture will slowly begin to change into a Problem-Solving culture and improvements in organizational performance will follow.

Typical Problem-Solving Languages

Problem-Solving Language	Recurring Problem Language
"We developed a detailed problem description"	"The customer said the problem is ..."
"We conducted a 5 Why Analysis"	"I filled out the 5 why analysis"
"The root cause is..."	"I think the root cause is..."
"This was a process failure related to..."	"This was an operator error caused by the operator on 2nd shift"
"Let's go to the process"	"Let's meet in my office"
"Operator involvement"	"Engineer-only involvement"

Figure 10.1 Problem Solving Language

Chapter 11

Problem-Solving Process Management

Problem Solving Review Team

A structured review of Problem Solving is a common characteristic of organizations with strong Problem-Solving cultures. The purpose for the Problem-Solving review team is to add a formal structure for monitoring progress and constraints experienced by the Problem-Solving teams. This type of weekly, or bi-weekly review does not take ownership for implementing the Problem-Solving process, as that needs to be owned by those responsible within the organizational units, or processes. Because of this, the Problem-Solving review team should not be implemented until the Problem-Solving process has been developed, trained, and implemented.

These reviews can be structured in many ways and can involve different levels of the organization. In my past as the Director of Quality in an OEM vehicle manufacturer we sent every problem that could lead to NHTSA filings such as field service actions, safety bulletins, or recalls. As the Quality Leader of a component parts manufacturer, we sent all problems that stemmed from safety incidents, customer concerns, or costly internal problems. As the Director of Quality at a different company, we sent all problems that were evaluated to rise above a certain risk level.

A useful tool to incorporate into the review team meetings is the use of a checklist. The checklist includes the highlights of what will typically be included in the Problem-Solving process. The checklist is useful for both the leadership group who is evaluating the Problem-Solving effort and it is also helpful for the Problem-Solving Team Leader and team members by providing a checklist of what to include in their final Problem-Solving package and presentation.

8-Step Evaluation Check List

Step 1: Validating the Problem and Selecting the Correct Approach
- Has the problem been validated as a real problem?
- Has an Emergency Action Plan been established?

Step 2: Team Member Selection and Recruitment
- Is the team identified?
- Is the team cross functional?
- Does the team include at least one user of the process?
- Does the team include 4-7 members?

Step 3: Problem Statement
- Is the problem statement clear and concise?
- Does it describe what is wrong with what?

Step 4: Containment & Temporary Corrective Actions
- Are containment methods appropriate?
- Was there a Quality/Safety Alert issued?
- Was a containment worksheet completed?
- Have affected personnel been trained?

Step 5: Root Cause Analysis
- Is there evidence that applicable Problem-Solving tools were used?
    - Work center observation and review
    - FMEA Review
    - Brainstorming
    - Cause & Effect diagram
    - 5 Why Analysis
- Is the stated root cause truly a root cause (rather than symptom or effect)?
- Does the root cause point to a person?
- Are all three legs of the 5 Why Analysis completed as appropriate?

Step 6: Permanent Corrective Action Identification, Selection, Implementation, Verification and Validation
- Was a PICK Chart or other method used to select the best options?
- Are all actions identified on an Action Plan?
    - Does timing appear appropriate?
        - Is necessary urgency indicated?
    - Do stated actions clearly address all root causes?

Step 7: Preventive Actions and Validation
- Was Design, Process, or Product FMEA updated?
- Was Control Plan reviewed/revised?
- Were process instructions reviewed/revised?

- Was training completed as necessary for changes implemented?
- Were Feed Across/Feed Forward opportunities identified, documented, and communicated?

Step 8: Celebrate Team Success

- Was the team recognized in some way?

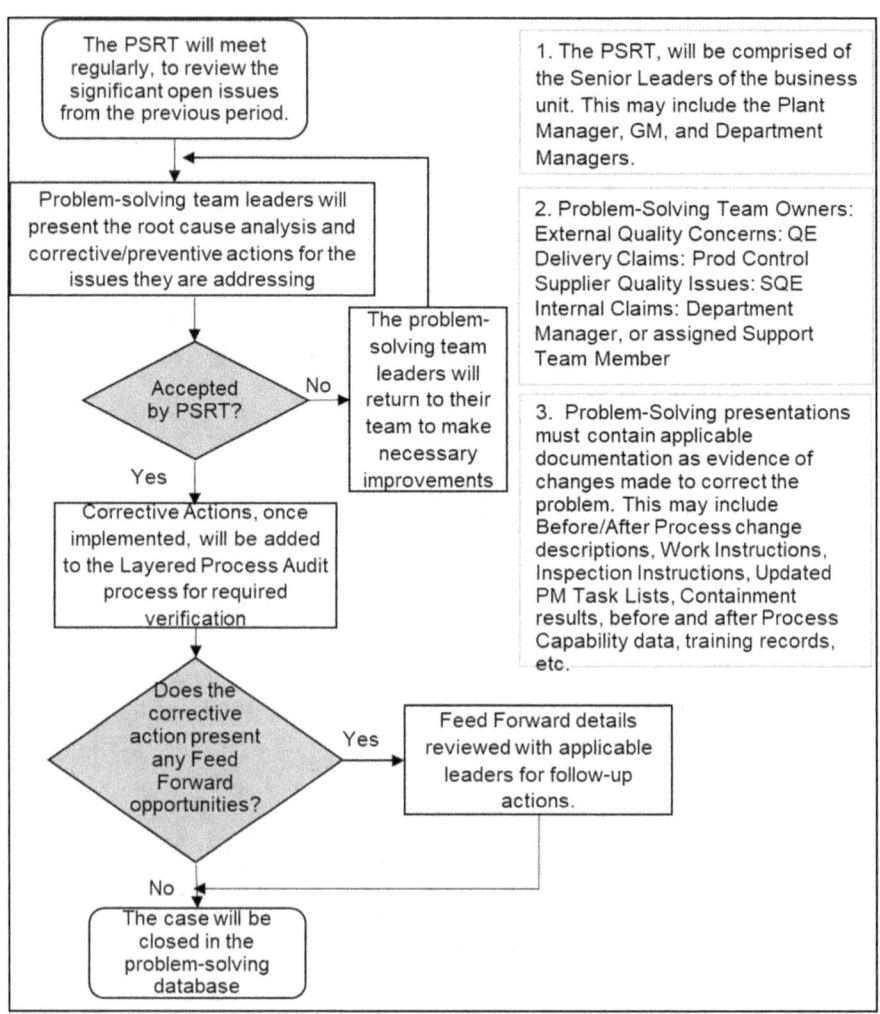

Figure 11.1 Problem Solving Review Team Process Map

Selected Problem-Solving Tools

5W/2H Tool (Used in Step 3)

The 5W2H tool is used to define information about the early understanding of a problem, or situation. In Problem Solving it is a great tool for summarizing known information to help create a problem statement. Unlike most of the other tools used in Problem Solving, the origins of the 5W2H tool goes back centuries where it was used as a formal means for questioning or surveying.

5W2H Instructions:

1. The team should review the problem statement.
2. The team must list all other information known to be factual about the problem.
3. Starting with the first question, ask all the questions until the team provides the best answer for every one that can be answered with the current level of understanding of the problem. (Leave the questions blank if they cannot be answered knowledgeably).
4. The team should try to find the answers to the blank questions and populate the rest of the matrix.
5. Once complete, the team will work to summarize the answers into a simple, accurate, concise statement.

	Questions	Answers
Who?	Who reported the problem?	Irish Poultry Products, Inc.
	Who is affected by the problem?	Irish Poultry Products, Inc.
What?	What has been reported as the problem?	Part number 123/XY – Creating noise and vibration in poultry feeder
When?	When was the problem first experienced?	May 12, 2018 at 3:47 PM
	When was it first reported?	May 12, 2018 at 3:47 PM
Where?	Where was the problem first experienced?	Irish Poultry Products, Inc.
	Where on the part was the problem?	Gear Teeth contact surface
Why?	Why is this a problem?	The noise/vibration in the feeder system distracted the chickens from eating
How many?	How many occurrences/units are involved?	1 pc
How big?	How big is the deviation from the requirement?	The noise level exceeded the design spec by 2.1dB

5 Why Analysis (Used in Step 5)

The 5 Why Analysis tool is very useful in drilling down from a high-level symptom down to the lowest level cause, (the root cause), for a problem. When used properly, the tool exhibits the concept that some of the biggest problems are initially caused by much smaller issues. It is important to note that there may be more or fewer than 5 Whys.

The concept of the 5 Why Analysis is simply taking the top-level issue and asking why in succession until it no longer makes sense to keep asking why. In practice however, it often takes time to search for answers to the whys. The 5 Why analysis often will not be completed in 5 minutes by asking and answering why 5 times in quick succession.

5 Whys Analysis Instructions:

1. Take the top potential cause from the Nominal Group Technique exercise and write it at the top of the whiteboard, or flipchart.
2. Read the top line and ask the first why.
3. Write the answer below the first why and ask the second why.
4. Repeat until it is no longer logical to ask why.
5. Verify the 5 Why analysis using the reverse logic, (therefore), test and by comparing it to the problem statement.

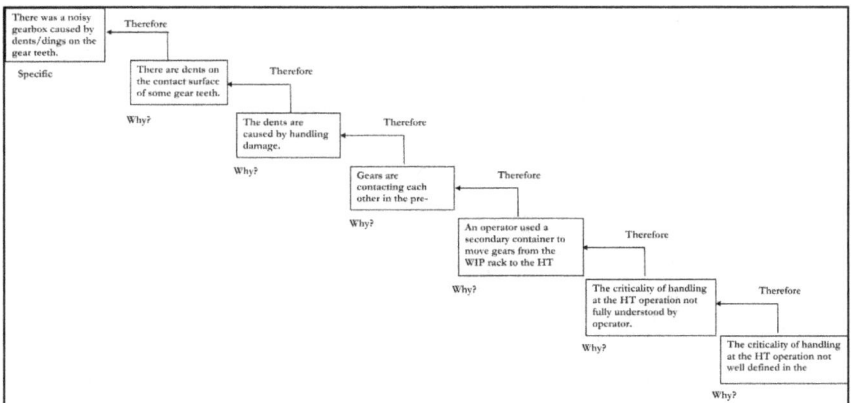

Action Plan (Used in Steps 1, 4, 6, & 7)

An action plan is as simple as it sounds. The reason for including it here is because even though it is very simple, it is also very important to the Problem-Solving team. The action plan establishes a record of actions and provides a vehicle for accountability.

Action Plan Instructions:

1. List all containment, improvement, corrective, and preventive actions in a simple matrix.
2. Record the date the action is due.
3. Record the date the action is completed.
4. Record an owner of each action. (Only one owner per action to ensure it is owned)
5. Review and update the action plan during team meetings.
6. If actions are changed, make a record of the reason it was changed.

No.	Action Item	C	CA	PA	Owner	Due	Actual
1.	Determine number of racks needed		X		WR	5/30/18	5/26/18
2.	Complete the design work to ensure the racks will work in all processes including Heat Treat		X		MM	6/11/18	6/12/18
3.	Outsource production of prototype rack to trial in process		X		FR	6/12/18	6/14/18
4.	Run trial through production processes using prototype rack		X		WR	7/13/18	7/15/18
5.	Outside source to complete build of all racks needed		X		PVW	9/10/18	9/08/18
6.	Complete work instructions to define proper use of new racks		X		PVW	8/3/18	8/13/18
7.	Feed Across corrective actions to the other production lines		X		WR	7/25/18	9/24/18
8.	Train affected employees in CAs		X		WR	9/13/18	9/13/18
C = Containment, CA = Corrective Action, PA = Preventive Action							

Benchmarking (Used in steps 5, 6, & 7)

The American Society for Quality, (ASQ), defines benchmarking as the process of measuring products, services, and processes against those of organizations known to be leaders in one or more aspects of their operations, (ASQ, 2021).

In the APQC Blog article titled What are the Four Types of Benchmarking, Mercy Harper, (Harper), list the four types of benchmarking below:

1. **Performance benchmarking**
2. **Practice benchmarking**
3. **Internal benchmarking**
4. **External benchmarking**

I have added some simple descriptions for each of the four below:

1. **Performance benchmarking:** involves gathering and comparing performance indicators such as KPIs and other metrics.
2. **Practice benchmarking:** Includes studying and reviewing comparable processes to identify better or best practices, or to provide an educated comparison.
3. **Internal benchmarking:** Includes reviewing processes, methods, solutions, and opportunities with other processes, departments, and business units within the same organization.
4. **External benchmarking:** Includes comparing product, processes, methods, and results with other organizations.

When it comes to most Problem-Solving activities, we are mostly talking about internal Benchmarking and what we are looking for is any opportunity to borrow an idea for root causes or corrective actions that may have affected another division, department, or line so we can shorten the time to figure out what does and does not work. It is a chance to learn from others, so we do not have to make the same mistakes.

Brainstorming (Used in Step 5)

There are many different types of Problem-Solving methods and there are pros and cons to each method. The method that seems to be used very often and is easy to use is a simple free-for-all approach where the team reviews the Problem Description and then randomly says their ideas if they have any and the facilitator records the ideas. Although this process usually takes just a few minutes, some leaders like to apply a time limit to the activity. I have not found it necessary to put a time limit on the activity, but I will put a secret time limit of 1 minute on the max amount of time since the last new idea. I will not share this ahead of time because I do not want to constrict the creativity of the team, but if 1-minute passes without any new ideas from the team, the team is likely done brainstorming.

Free-for-all Brainstorming Instructions:

1. Define and agree to the objective.
2. Review the Problem Description to refresh the parameters for the team.
3. Brainstorm ideas and suggestions having an agreed upon time limit.
    a. (A time limit is generally not necessary when doing a free-for-all approach as the facilitator needs to know to stop it when the flow of ideas stops, which normally takes no more than a few minutes.)
4. The facilitator, or scribe will record the ideas on a flipchart, or whiteboard.
5. Categorize/condense/combine/refine the ideas.

May 16, 2018

Forrester Agricultural Products – Chicken Feeder

Brainstorming List
- Parts were dropped
- Parts were damaged in hobbing process
- Parts were damaged during inspection
- Parts were damaged while being moved
- Parts were damaged during assembly
- Parts were damaged during broaching
- Parts were damaged during loading onto racks
- Operator not trained
- Operator failed to follow process
- Parts being hit at the process during maintenance activities

Problem Statement

"On May 12, 2018, Forrester Agricultural Products, Inc. reported 1 gearbox of P/N 123-XYZ produced on May 5, 2018, with excessive noise due to dents/dings on gear teeth contact surface"

Capability Study & Analysis (Used in Step 7)

Capability analysis is simply a graphical and numerical means by evaluating the capability of a process. The information obtained from this type of evaluation is very useful in determining whether a process is capable of meeting the specifications and it is useful in evaluating levels of process improvement over time. There are various types of capability analyses, but the most commonly used format is one that assumes the data is variable and the distribution is normal.

There are two commonly used capability indices used to evaluate how capable a process is and they both rely on the mean and standard deviation from the data and the specification limits from the process or product feature. The 2 common capability indices are Cpk, and CP.

Capability Study & Analysis Instructions:
1. Collect data based on a rational sample size, (30+ samples)
2. Determine whether the process data demonstrates a state of statistical control (Since the process is in control, there will be no presence of special cause variation)
3. Enter the data into a statistical analysis software for the calculations. If statistical analysis software is not available, the formulas for the calculations can easily be created in a spreadsheet or they can be done with a pen and paper and a simple calculator.
    a. Cpk: (min value of either) $\underline{\frac{USL-AVG, \text{ or } AVG-LSL}{3\sigma}}$
    b. Cp: $\underline{\frac{USL-LSL}{6\sigma}}$
4. The higher the value from these calculations, the more capable the process.

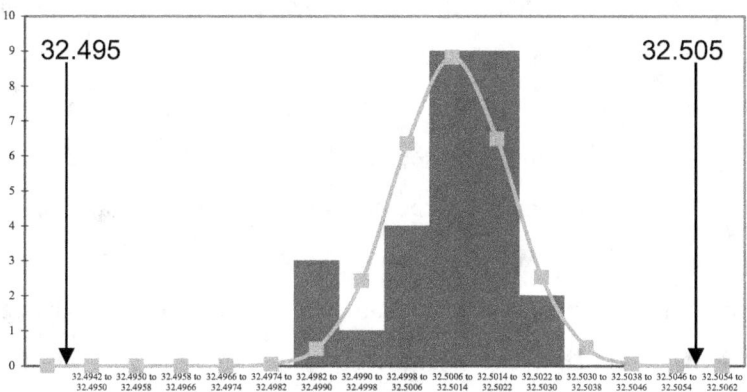

Figure 12.1 Capability Study

```
Cp 2.091236
Cpk 1.688469
```

Cause & Effect Diagram (Used in Step 5)

The Cause & Effect Diagram is also known as the Ishikawa Diagram and the Fishbone Diagram. The diagram is typically used during the root cause analysis step in the Problem-Solving process and is typically used in conjunction with brainstorming. As seen in the example below, the diagram is divided into categories based on themes, to organize the data. Cause & Effect Diagrams will typically have 4 categories used to categorize the data from the brainstorming activity, but some may have 6, or even 8 categories.

Cause & Effect Diagram Instructions:

1. Enter the problem statement in the box at the right.
2. Enter the ideas on the diagram under the appropriate category.
3. Once all ideas are entered, see if the team can come up with additional ideas based on the ideas listed and enter them on branches coming off the original ideas.
4. Once all ideas are entered, begin to narrow them down by likelihood of occurrence. Strikethrough the ideas that are most unlikely, but do not erase the ideas as they may be reviewed again later.
5. Next, categorize the remaining ideas by each of the three legs of the root cause analysis.

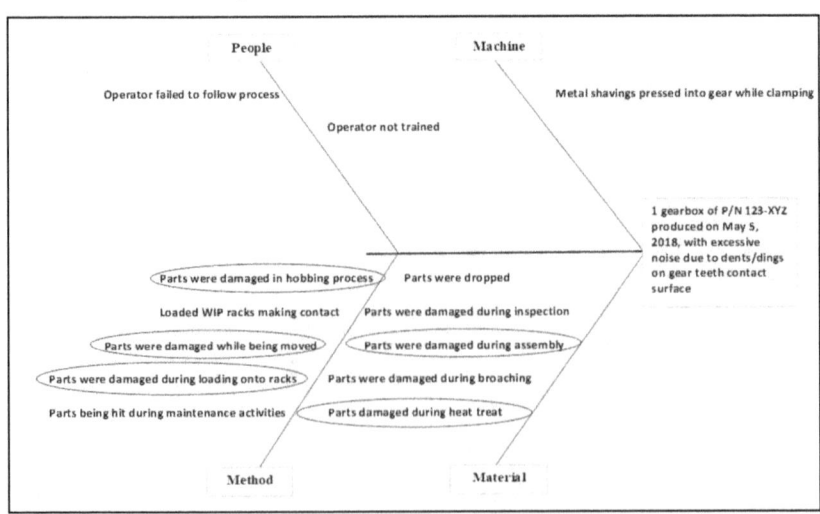

Check Sheet (Used in Steps 1, 4, and 7)

The check sheet is one of the original 7 basic Quality tools. It is simply a method to collect data for data analysis and is often used for an inspection record. It is often set up with several product or process characteristics to be monitored using some prescribed technique. Once the inspection or observation has been made, a record of it will be entered onto the check sheet. This typically continues at prescribed frequencies and the check sheet is typically turned in to someone at the end of a shift, or workday. The check sheet in the example below was created to record and collect inspection data from a containment activity.

Check Sheet Instructions:

1. Determine the features or characteristics that need inspected or monitored.
2. Create and control a form for data collection.
3. Define the frequency and any special instructions for the activity and enter the information on the check sheet.
4. Train affected associates in the use of the check sheet.
5. Review collected/completed check sheets to analyze the data.
6. Provide feedback to the affected associates regarding the results and any concerns over the data collection.

Forrester Agricultural Products, Inc. Containment Checksheet							
Date:	12-May-18			Issue Leader:	Natalie Forrester		
Part Number(s):	123-XYZ						
Issue Description:	Gear Teeth found with Dents/Dings						

Box/Lot Number	Box Qty	Excessive Dings/Dent	Defects Other (Burrs)	Defects Other (rust)	Responsible for Verification	Actions taken	Date
Example (Lot 042218-1)	72	1	0	0	Scott B.	Stoned flat the Dents/Dings	5/12/2018
Lot 042218-1	72	16	1	0	Audra F.	Replaced part with known good part	5/12/2018
Lot 042218-2	72	9	0	0	Colin B.		5/12/2018
Lot 042218-3	72	12	0	0	Braxston F.	Stoned flat the Dents/Dings	5/12/2018
Lot 042218-4	72	14	0	0	Delani L.		5/12/2018
Lot 042218-5	72	9	0	0	Kairi W.	Stoned flat the Dents/Dings	5/12/2018
Lot 042218-6	60	3	0	0	Weston W.	Stoned flat the Dents/Dings	5/12/2018
Lot 042218-7	72	0	0	0	Callum F.		5/12/2018
Lot 042218-8	72	2	0	0	Malcolm F.	Stoned flat the Dents/Dings	5/12/2018
Totals per Shift	564	65	1	0			

Turn in checksheet to QC office at the end of each shift
Reaction Plan for Defects Identified: Contact QA Mgr immediately if "other" defects found (other than primary containment reason).

Containment Worksheet (Used in Steps 1 and 4)

The containment worksheet is a tool that is used to ensure that all potentially affected population of product that could be defective is accounted for. The containment worksheet is populated using inventory data from the related processes and the ERP inventory management system.

Containment Worksheet Instructions:

1. Identify every possible inventory location throughout the process and record on the Containment Worksheet.
2. Determine the inventory expected at each location by reviewing the ERP system, or other inventory system.
3. Perform a physical count to ensure the physical number matches the expected number from the ERP system. (If there is a difference between the quantity listed in the inventory system and the physical count, the numbers must be reconciled.)
4. Enter the inventory quantities in the Containment Worksheet.
5. Once the inventory quantities are reconciled and all inventory is quarantined, the physical inspection can be started.
6. Record the containment results and dates on the Containment worksheet and keep as part of the Problem-Solving record.

Forrester Agricultural Products, Inc. Containment Worksheet

Date: 12-May-18 Issue Lead: Natalie Forrester
Part Number(s): 123-XYZ
Issue Description: Dents/Dings found on Gear Teeth

Location / Area	ERP Qty	Actual Qty	Qty Pass	Qty Fail	Required Action	Date
Shipping Area	288	288	288	0		5/12/2018
Receiving Area	0	0	0	0		5/12/2018
In Transit from Supplier	0	0	0	0		5/12/2018
Component Cell(s)	326	326	326	0		5/12/2018
Assembly Cell(s)/Line(s)	0	0	0	0		5/12/2018
Hold Area	0	0	0	0		5/12/2018
Warehouse	1728	1728	1728	0		5/12/2018
Staged for truck	0	0	0	0		5/12/2018
In Transit to Customer	0	0	0	0		5/12/2018
At Customer	1728	1728	1727	1	1. Issued RMA to customer and will contain product once received at FAPI. 2. Tag rejected part and send to QA lab for further analysis	5/14/2018
At Outside Processor	0	0	0	0		5/12/2018
Samples in QA Lab	6	6	6	0		5/12/2018
1st Article Board at Machine Cells	4	4	4	0		5/12/2018
Other Loc.						
Other Loc.						

Total Inventory Qty: 4080 | 4080 Note: The SAP Qty and the Actual Qty MUST match! If there is a variance, follow the reaction plan below.

Reaction Plan for Inventory Discrepancy: Contact both the QA Mgr and the Materials Planning Mgr immediately to determine next course of action.

Control Plan (Used in steps 5, 6, & 7)

A Control Plan is a formally controlled, living document that is used to define and control product features and characteristics as well as the process parameters that generate, or affect those product features. The Control Plan is linked to the FMEA as the FMEA identifies which process and product features need to be controlled.

The Control Plan is set-up for three phases of development: the prototype phase, the pre-launch phase, and the production phase. This is generally necessary because the needs and requirements for controls changes at all three phases.

Structurally, the Control Plan follows the process flow and describes the process steps, the key product features being generated and controlled in those steps, the methods of control, the frequency of control and a reaction plan to follow if there is an issue identified. The information contained in the Control Plan makes it very useful when Problem Solving and especially when analyzing the Why Not Detected root cause.

The information contained in the control plan makes it very helpful when establishing process audits as the controls for any particular process step are contained within one easy to follow document.

☐ Prototype	☐ Pre-Launch	☑ Production		CONTROL PLAN							
Control Plan Number			Key Contact/Phone Tracy Forrester				Date (Orig.) 2/18/2016		Date (Rev.) 7/22/2018		
Part Number/Latest Change Level 123/XYZ			Core Team				Customer Engineering Approval/Date (If Req'd.) N/A				
Part Name/Description Spur Gear			Supplier/Plant Approval/Date				Customer Quality Approval/Date (If Req'd.) N/A				
PART/ PROCESS NUMBER	PROCESS NAME/ OPERATION DESCRIPTION	MACHINE, DEVICE JIG, TOOLS FOR MFG.	CHARACTERISTICS		SPECIAL CHAR. CLASS	METHODS					REACTION PLAN
			NO.	PRODUCT/ PROCESS		PRODUCT/PROCESS SPECIFICATION/ TOLERANCE	EVALUATION/ MEASUREMENT TECHNIQUE	SAMPLE		RESPONSIBLE FOR MEAS.	CONTROL METHOD	
								SIZE	FREQ.			
Spur Gears	Internal Spline	N/A	17	Gear Teeth Dents	N/A	No dents on gear contact surface larger than size 2	Visual	3 Pcs	Per Hr	Operator	Document on Check Sheet	Quarantine suspect/defective gears Contact Team Leader
	Hobbing						Mylar Dent Size Chart	1	As needed	Operator	Document on Check Sheet	Quarantine suspect/defective gears Contact Team Leader
	Inspection											
	Heat Treat											

Error Proofing/Mistake Proofing Used in steps 6 & 7)

What is mistake proofing? Mistake proofing is another term for Poka-yoke, which is a Japanese term that translates to inadvertent error prevention. The American Society for Quality, (ASQ), defines mistake proofing as "the use of any automatic device or method that either makes it impossible for an error to occur or makes the error immediately obvious once it has occurred".

The main purpose for including a discussion about mistake proofing here is that mistake proofing should always be considered in the Problem-Solving process when determining and implementing various corrective and preventive actions.

There are two primary categories of Mistake Proofing:
1. Warnings/Alarms – provides information
2. Controls – prevents and/or stops the process

Within the two categories of Mistake Proofing there are three basic types:
1. Contact method - identifies defects by testing product characteristics. Commonly used for presence, position, and orientation.
2. Fixed-value - a specific number of movements, repeated every time.
3. Sequence method – Every task completed in the correct order. Determines if the process was followed.

Hierarchy of the reliability of different approaches to Mistake Proofing

BEST
Prevent defects from occurring at all.

BETTER
Detects defects while in process at an operation.

GOOD
Detect defect before proceeding to next step.

Feed Across/Feed Forward (Used in Steps 1 & 7)

Feed Across/Feed Forward is a critical proactive measure to ensure that the same issue does not occur beyond the original incident. Specifically, the tool is used to ensure the same or a similar issue does not occur on another product, in another process, or in another location.

Feed Across/Feed Forward is a tool that can be used at the following opportunities to apply the containment, corrective, and preventive actions.

Feed Across/Feed Forward Instructions

1. Review the list of root causes, containment actions, and corrective/preventive actions with the team.
2. Review the following list of potential FA/FF opportunities:
   a. Additional customer locations (External)
   b. Additional supplier locations (External)
   c. Additional business locations (Internal)
   d. Additional departments (Internal)
   e. Additional processes (Internal)
   f. Additional products or services (Internal)
3. If the team identifies opportunities, communicate with the leadership from those areas to share the applicable actions taken.

Forrester Agricultural Products, Inc. - Feed Across/Feed Forward

Origin of Issue		Feed Forward			Feed Across													
					External			Internal										
		Lessons Learned Database	Process Design Stds for Safe Gear Handling	Risk Analysis Std for FMEA Development	Customer Loc 1 (Original)	Customer Loc 2	Supplier Loc 1	Supplier Loc 2	Internal Ship/Dept/Function 1 Internal	Ship/Dept/Function 2 Internal	Ship/Dept/Function 3 Internal	Machine/Process 1	Machine/Process 2	Machine/Process 3	Machine/Process 4	Machine/Process 5	Part/Project No: 1 (123-XYZ)	Part/Project No: 2	Part/Project No: 3
Date of Issue: 12-May-18																		
Customer: Irish Poultry Products																		
Internal Dept: Gear Manufacturing																		
Part #: 1213-XYZ																		
Problem Statement: On May 12, 2018, Irish Poultry Products, Inc. reported 1 gearbox of P/N 123-XYZ produced on May 5, 2018, with excessive noise due to dents/dings on gear teeth contact surface																		
Defect: Dents/Damage on Gear Teeth																		
Root Cause(s):	Gear Mfg process not adequately defined	A		A					O			A	A	O	A	A	O	A	A
Containment Action(s):	Sort all product visually and with mylar defect template					O				O			A	A	O	A	A	O	A	A
Corrective/ Preventive Action(s):	Design common gear racks to reduce handling damage	A	A							O			A	A	O	A	A	O	A	A
O = Original Process for the issue, containment, or corrective/preventive actions. A = Applicable Process for the issue, containment, or corrective/preventive actions																		

FMEA (Used in steps 5, 6, & 7)

Failure Mode Effects Analysis is a qualitative risk analysis of failures and a study of their effects on various components, sub-systems, systems, processes, and designs. Once an evaluation has been completed using standard, (or customized), ranking values for the Severity, Occurrence, and Detection of the failures, teams can work to reduce the risk by improving designs and processes.

The combined rankings from the Severity, Occurrence, and Detection of the failure are used to establish the overall Risk Priority Number, (RPN), as a relative measure of overall risk.

An FMEA is an analytical tool that uses a disciplined technique to identify and help eliminate potential product and process failure modes.

- By identification of potential failures
- Assessing the risks associated with failure modes and identifying corrective actions
- Prioritizing corrective actions
- Carrying out corrective actions

The FMEA is primarily developed prior to the design and production processes, but due to the structured nature and relative ease of use, FMEAs can be used to identify points of risk for any type of process including safety, transactional, service, inspection systems, audit systems, single process steps or for expansive and complex processes.

FMEAs are living documents and should always be reviewed and updated during the Problem Solving and Change Management processes.

FMEA														
Part Name: Hub Part Number: 123-XYZ			Date (Orig): 3/21/17 Date (Rev): 8/15/18					Owner: Lathe Process Eng.						
Product or Process	Failure Mode	Failure Effects	Causes	Controls	SEV	OCC	DET	RPN	Action Recommended	Action Taken	PS	PO	PD	RPN
Hub - CNC Lathe Process	Diameter undersize	Mating component fits loosely	Improper/missed tool change	Inspection following tool change	7	4	5	140	5/12/18 - Forrester Automotive had 1 pc with undersize diameter by -.015.mm 1. Implement Auto-offset program to remove risk of not making the correct offset following a tool change 2. Implement auto gaging to detect future dimensional failures.	1. Implement Auto-offset program to remove risk of not making the correct offset following a tool change 2. Implemented in-line gaging to auto inspect the diameter.	7	2	3	42

The tables below consist of commonly suggested ranking scales for the FMEA. The ranking scales include rankings from 1 thru 10 for each of the three areas of risk which consist of the Severity of the failure, the rate of Occurrence of the failure, and the probability of Detecting the failure. The rankings are generic, and it is always recommended that the scales be customized to suit the specific needs of the organization and function developing the FMEA.

PFMEA Severity Scale	
Severity Rank	Description
10	Hazardous, without warning
9	Hazardous, with warning
8	Very High
7	High
6	Moderate
5	Low
4	Very Low
3	Minor
2	Very Minor
1	None

PFMEA Occurrence Scale	
Occurrence Rank	Description
10	>100 Per 1,000
9	50 Per 1,000
8	20 Per 1,000
7	10 Per 1,000
6	5 Per 1,000
5	2 Per 1,000
4	1 Per 1,000
3	0.5 Per 1,000
2	0.1 Per 1,000
1	< 0.01 Per 1,000

PFMEA Detection Scale	
Detection Rank	Description
10	Absolutely Impossible
9	Very Remote
8	Remote
7	Very Low
6	Low
5	Moderate
4	Moderately High
3	High
2	Almost Certain
1	Certain

Gage R & R Study (Used in Steps 5 & 6)

Gage R&R studies, or Measurement Systems Analyses, are statistical analyses that are conducted to evaluate the usefulness of gages and measurement systems. A gage R&R study can be conducted on both variable and attribute measurement systems.

When measuring the product from any process, there are two sources of variation: the variation of the process itself and the variation of the measurement system. The purpose for conducting the GR&R study is to be able to differentiate between the two. Gage R&R studies are particularly helpful when evaluating new measurement systems, or in reaction to a process capability problem. If the process capability is low, it is important to determine how much of the variation is from the measurement system before spending unnecessary resources on improving the process.

The "R&R" portion of gage R&R stands for Repeatability and Reproducibility.

Repeatability: Known as the Equipment Variation and is the measurement of the ability to repeat measurements using the same gage and operator.

Reproducibility: Known as the Appraiser Variation and is the measurement of the ability of two or, more operators to get consistent measurements on the same parts using the same gage.

The variable studies are typically conducted with 10 parts, 3 operators and for 3 trials each.

Acceptance Criteria for Measurement Systems Analysis (MSA)
1. If the % **Gage R&R** is under 10%, the measurement system is generally considered to be an adequate measurement system.
2. If the % **Gage R&R** is between 10 % to 30%, the measurement system may be acceptable for some applications.
3. If the % **Gage R&R** is over 30%, the measurement system is considered to be unacceptable.

For Attribute Studies, the study is typically conducted with 30-50 parts, (including both good and bad parts), with 3 operators, and run for 3 trials each. The criteria for the individual tests are pass/fail.

The statistical analysis can be quite difficult and is typically completed with various statistical software like Minitab or with an MS Excel add-in.

Gemba Walk (Used in any/all steps)

Gemba, (or Genba), is a Japanese word meaning "the actual place". This is what former Toyota Chief Engineer Taiichi Ohno was talking about when he said, "use your feet to investigate processes and not your computer", (Liker, 258). This is also what we are talking about in step 3 of the List of Common Steps for Conducting a Root Cause Analysis, which is "Go to the process".

There are many advantages to spending time at Gemba and for conducting regularly planned Gemba reviews by leadership. Some advantages may include:

- Seeing first-hand what is really happening in the process
- Interaction with the process owners and process users
- Following up on changes
- Promoting open communication
- Reinforcement of policies and standards

Some keys to remember about Gemba walks:

1. Safety always! All participants must always practice and reinforce proper safety protocol.
2. The purpose for the Gemba walk may be specific, or it may be a general review. Discuss the purpose and plans for the walk prior to going to Gemba.
3. All involved must demonstrate respect for all who are encountered during the walk.
4. Stay together as a group.
5. Follow the process.
6. Ask questions.
7. Do not offer suggestions for changes during the walk.
8. Take notes if allowed.
9. Regroup with the team after the walk to discuss findings.

Layered Process Audit (Used in steps 7 & 8)

"Layered Process Audits require that multiple operational levels within a manufacturing facility review the same key operational controls (within the reviewer's span of authority) that ensure product quality" (AIAG, 2014).

Layered Process Audits, (LPAs), are process audits that are conducted by layers of an organization. The term "layers" refers to multiple levels, (or layers), of the personnel in an organization. Some organizations that conduct LPAs differ in their views on some of the elements including how the layers are defined and what the layers do. When implementing LPAs in several organizational BUs, I have defined layers as outlined below:

Layer 1 – Executive Team (Directors, VPs, President)

Layer 2 – Dept. Managers and other Management

Layer 3 – Supervisors and Engineer

Layer 4 – Hourly (QA Tech, Operator, etc.)

Many organizations vary the scale of the audits that are conducted by different layers, but it is advantageous to have all layers conducting the same audits. There are many reasons for this, but given the brevity of LPAs, (never longer than 15 minutes), and the obvious value in doing them, I have not been able to find a reason to have different layers doing different audits.

LPAs include auditing various items in an organization including:

- Safety related items
- Customer Complaint History
- Quality Alerts
- Process stability and capability – Presence of special cause variation and low capability indices like Cp/Cpk
- First Pass Yield – rework/scrap
- PFMEA - High RPN Values
- Error-proofing /detection
- Implemented Corrective Actions Verification
- Operator Training Verification

- Implemented Changes/Improvements Verification

Monthly audit reports are distributed to leadership. Serious, systemic, or recurring findings are reported on and tracked in plant leadership meetings. LPA issues and resulting corrective actions may become Lessons Learned. LPA results should always be reviewed as part of Management Review.

Some of the many benefits to implementing LPAs include:

- LPAs lead to improvements in safety, quality, and other areas.
- LPAs are conducted by all levels of plant associates including the President.
- LPAs identify areas where improvements are necessary to prevent problems.
- Improvements are made immediately for individual findings and systemically for recurring findings.

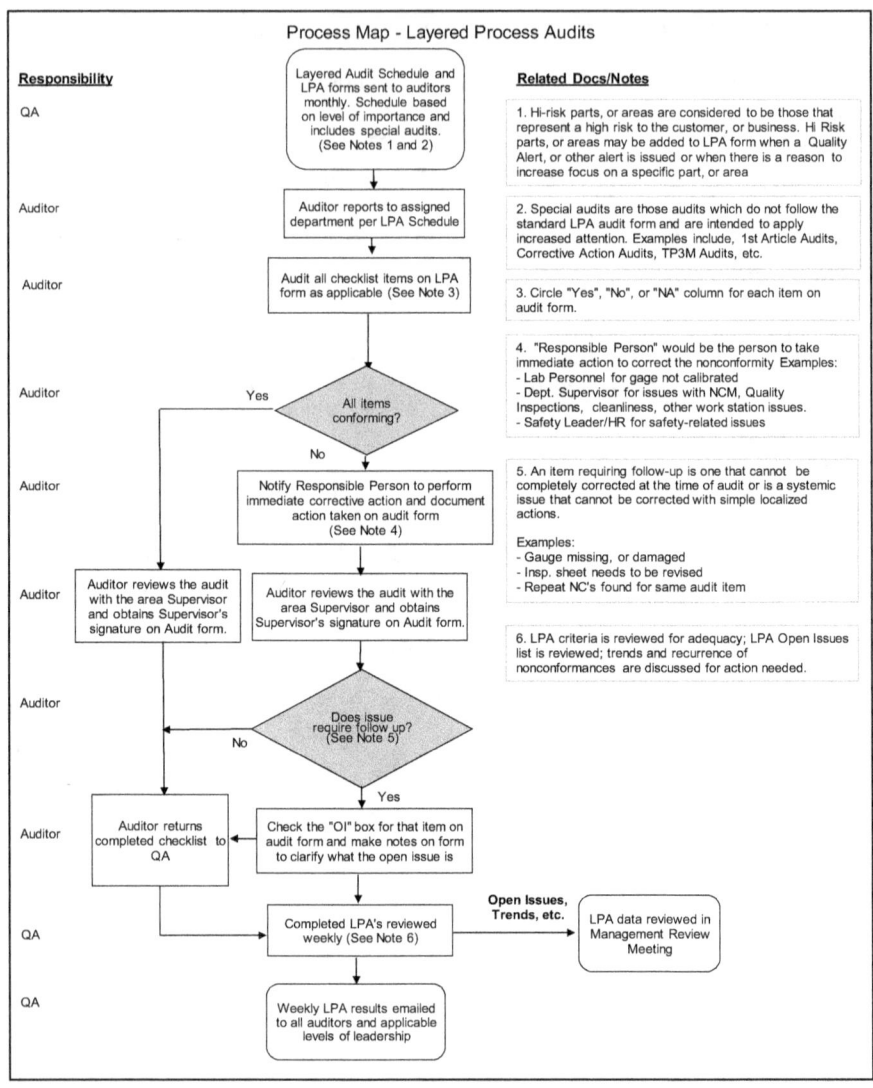

Figure 12.2 Layered Process Audit Map

Lessons Learned (Used in steps 5, 6, 7 & 8)

Lessons learned is a method for capturing and improving from lessons learned when reviewing the elements of a project in hindsight. This often includes a formal review and a listing of "Things Gone Right", (TGR), and "Things Gone Wrong", (TGW). The general intent is to document these lessons learned and then review and discuss the list in the future prior to initiating the next project. The purpose is to prevent the problems from recurring on the next project and to experience the good things on the next project.

The Project Management Institute includes a formal series of steps for the process:

Step 1: Identify comments and suggestions.

Step 2: Document the findings.

Step 3: Analyze the findings and lessons.

Step 4: Store the lessons learned in some retrievable method.

Step 5: Retrieve the information when it is time to plan for the next project.

This is the generally accepted method for identifying and applying lessons learned. If following this approach for lessons learned, ideally there will be a searchable database that can be searched on key words and phrases.

Another way to accomplish this that typically places less active burden on the system user is to identify what went wrong and apply problem solving to whichever process it applies, and to make permanent changes to the process going forward. One preference is to take the improvements and build those into the process as well. In other words, focus on institutionalizing the improvements into the process, which will eliminate the need to keep these lessons on lists somewhere and to rely on someone to review the list during the next project.

Measles Chart (Used in Steps 5 & 7)

A measles chart is also known as a defect concentration diagram. The purpose for using a measles chart in a Quality application is to show where defects are occurring on a visual of the product or process. Measles charts may be used in Quality on products, complex assemblies, or even locations throughout a business.

The example below shows where water leaks were located during a study of 100 delivery vehicles. Aside from a few leaks in the front around the windshield area, most of the leaks were concentrated around the rear roll-up door and surrounding structure. Looking at the data in this way provided great information for the Quality and Engineering teams to know where to focus their improvement efforts.

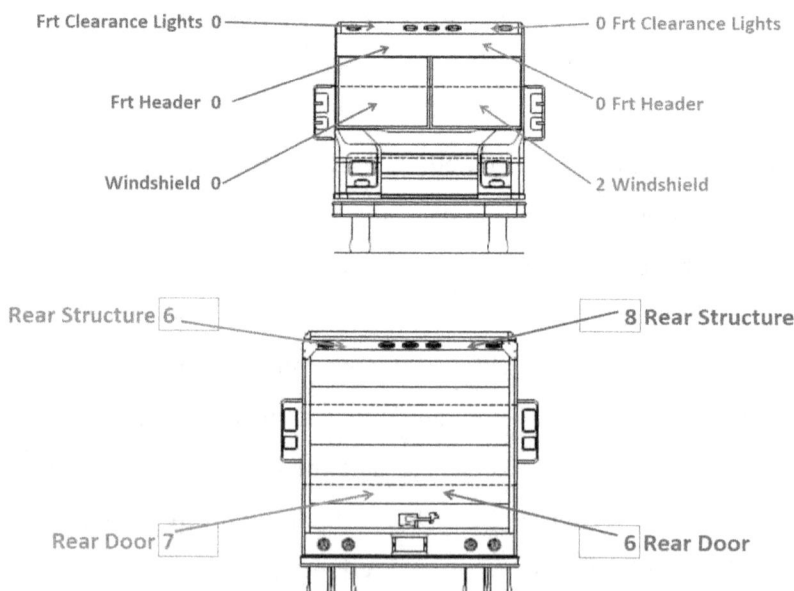

Figure 12.3 Measles Chart

Another approach to a measles chart is to simply take a process map and add defect rates to the steps in the process where the defects occur.

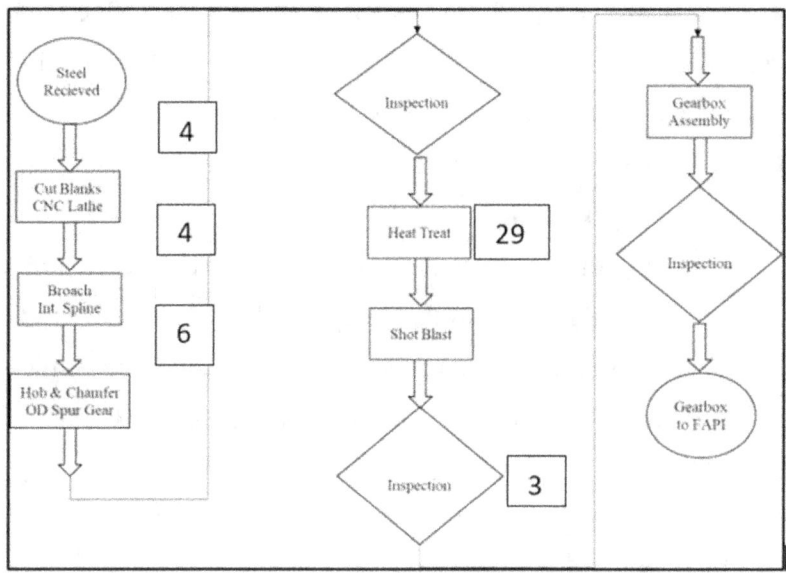

Nominal Group Technique (Used in Step 5)

The Nominal Group Technique, (NGT), is a structured method used in the root cause analysis step of Problem Solving to determine which potential cause to focus on first. It is a way to narrow down several potential causes to one that the team can start with. As is the case with the rest of the Problem-Solving process, NGT is a team-based method.

Nominal Group Technique

1. Generating Ideas: If a brainstorming session has been completed, the ideas generated from that session will be used for the NGT. If no brainstorming has been completed, the moderator reads the problem statement to the group and writes it on the board. Each person will present their ideas aloud.
2. Recording Ideas: Write the ideas from the team on a whiteboard, or flip chart that is visible to the entire team. Proceed until all members' ideas have been documented.
3. Discussing Ideas: Discuss each recorded idea to clarify and determine relative importance. This step provides an opportunity for team members to share their understanding of and the relative importance of the item.
4. Voting on Ideas: Individuals vote privately using sticky notes, to prioritize the ideas.

Each team member selects the 5 most important items from the group list and writes one idea on each sticky note along with their rank number for that idea, (1-5).

In the example provided, the team carried over 5 ideas from their brainstorming, so they voted 1-5 on each of the items, with 1 being their assessment of the most likely cause. Once the voting was completed, the results were populated into the matrix and the potential cause with the lowest total was deemed to be the most likely cause. From there, the team will start their 5 why analysis with that potential cause.

Potential Cause from Brainstorming/Cause & Effect Diagram	Team Member	Team Member	Team Member	Team Member	Team Member	Totals	Ranking
	Results on voting from each team member on each potential cause						
Parts Damaged in Hobbing	2	4	3	5	4	18	4
Parts Damaged When Moved	3	3	4	2	3	15	3
Parts Damaged During Assy	4	1	2	1	2	10	2
Parts Damaged During HT	1	2	1	3	1	8	(1)
Parts Damaged While Loaded	5	5	5	4	5	24	5

Pareto Diagram (Used in Steps 3, 5 & 7)

The Pareto diagram is a prioritization tool that is used to separate "the vital few from the trivial many". The Pareto diagram was created in 1897 by Italian economist Vilfredo Pareto. Pareto's observation was that 80 percent of the wealth was possessed by 20 percent of the people. Since the Pareto diagram was first introduced, many people have applied the principle to other applications such as ranking the frequency of defects and errors.

The Pareto Diagram is especially useful because it provides a visual prioritization through a simple comparative analysis. The majority of improvement initiatives will always be focused on the top 1-3 bars of the Pareto Diagram.

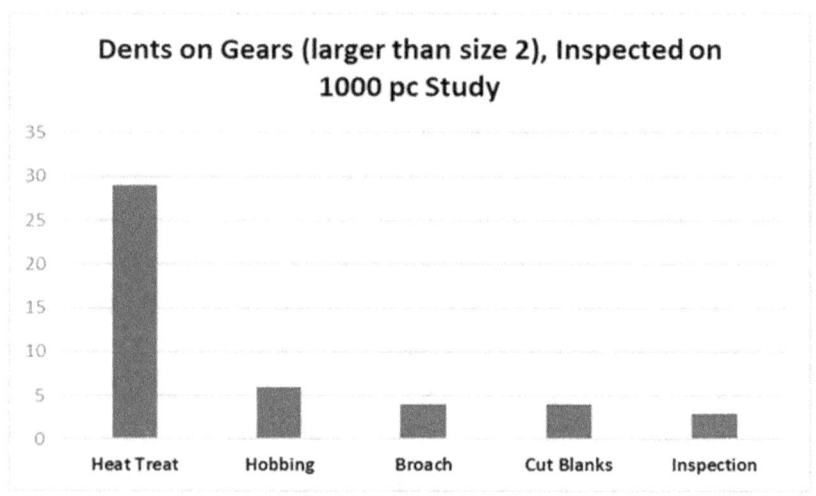

PICK Chart (Used in Steps 6 & 7)

A PICK chart is a project prioritization tool that was first created by Lockheed Martin and is used to differentiate projects and solutions based on their perceived *impact* and expected *effort* to implement. The highest priority is placed on those items that will require the lowest effort but will yield the greatest impact. (Note: If the team does not have a good understanding of the approximate Impact/Effort of solutions, they will need to consult with the Champion, or other sources of knowledge to establish a scale for each axis).

- **Potential:** includes the ideas that are easy to implement and with a low impact.
- **Implement:** for projects that are easy to implement, with a potentially high impact.
- **Check:** includes projects that may have a high impact but require a high effort. Some further investigation may need to be done to determine whether to pursue.
- **Kill:** eliminates ideas that are hard to implement and with a low return.

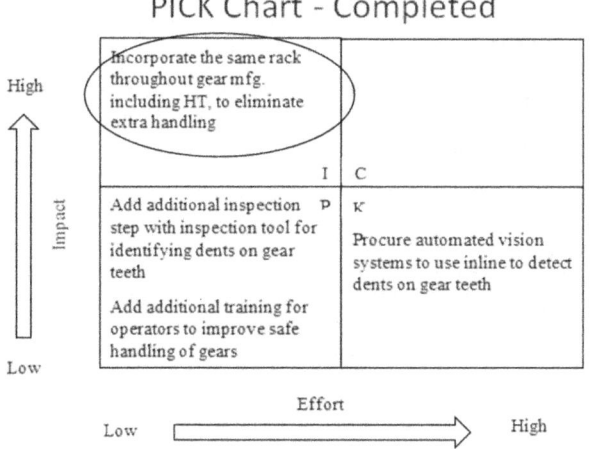

Process Flow Chart (Used in all Steps)

A flow chart is a simple, yet sometimes invaluable tool for Problem Solving. A flow chart is a simple visual diagram that shows a linear sequence of process steps from beginning to end. Flow charts are particularly helpful in understanding where problems may occur, where containment and corrective actions should be implemented, and flow charts may help to determine where to apply Feed Across/Feed Forward preventive actions.

If a flow chart does not exist for a process, they are easy for anyone to create.

Flow Chart Development Instructions:
1. Determine the process for the flow chart development.
2. Establish the boundaries around the beginning and end of the process, (the first and last steps).
3. Work with process owners, or process users to identify the linear sequence of each step in the process. (Some judgement may be needed to determine which steps are significant and which are less significant and which of these to include).
4. Write the process steps on sticky notes and post on a wall. (Be sure to include significant decisions and feedback loops where helpful).
5. Once all steps are identified and the sequence is correct, draw the flow chart in a computer program that is available to team members and to other interested parties.

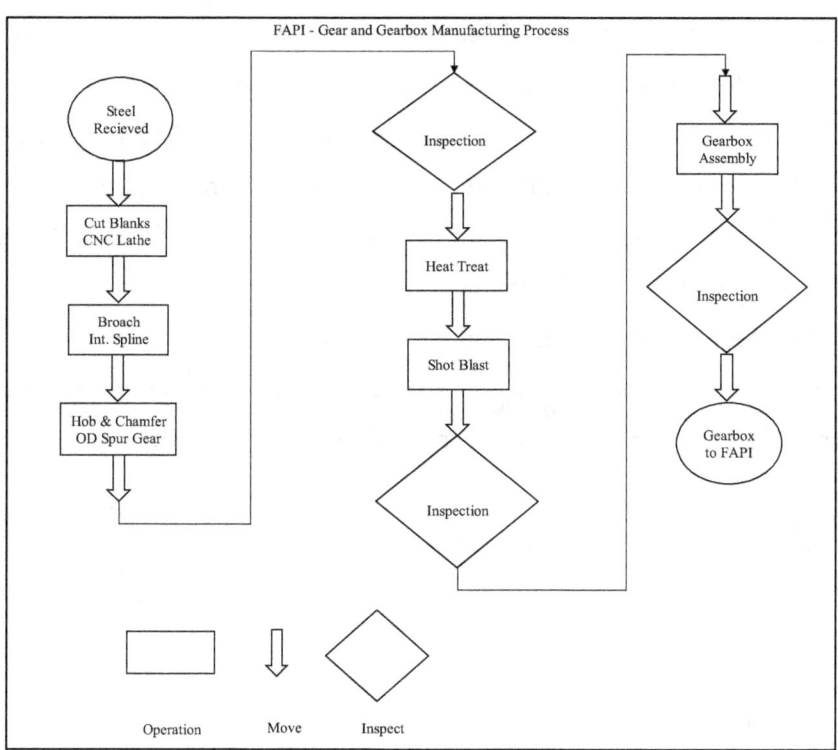

RASIC Matrix (Used in Step 2)

One of the struggles that are eventually experienced by most teams is making sure there are clearly defined roles and responsibilities. One way to avoid this problem is to clearly define the roles and responsibilities up front, when the team is formed. The purpose for using the **RASIC** tool is to identify responsibilities of all team members.

Populating the matrix is as simple as listing the roles of the team on the X axis and the responsibilities of the team members on the Y axis. Then, simply put the corresponding letter from the key in the matrix where it belongs.

RASIC Matric for Problem-Solving Team	Champion	Leader	Scribe	Timekeeper	Team Members	Process Owner
Recruit/Assign Team Members	A	R	I			C
Keep Team Focused	S	R	S	S	S	
Applying & Teaching Problem Solving	S	R				
Keeping Mtgs on Track to Time		A	S	R	S	
Provide Necessary Resources	R	S				
Manage Constraints to the Team	R	S				S
Keeping & Distributing Mtg Notes	I	A	R	I	I	
Provide Technical Input	C	A	S	S	R	C
Collect Data		A	S	S	R	S
Analyze Data	C	A	S	S	R	
Identify Solutions	C	A	S	S	R	S
Implement Solutions	I	S	S	S	S	R

R = Responsible

Those who do the work to complete the task.

A = Accountable

The one ultimately answerable for the deliverable or task

S = Support

Provides support to the team. Helps complete the task.

I = Informed

Those who are kept up to date on progress

C = Consulted

Those whose opinions are sought, typically subject matter experts

Trend Chart (Used in Steps 1, 3, 5, 6, & 7)

A trend chart is a simple chart that is used to plot data over time. As use of the word "trend" implies, the primary value of the trend chart is to determine whether a process result, or output is changing over time. A common use for trend charts in Problem Solving is to see whether something in a process has changed, (got better or worse), either prior to Problem Solving or to validate the effectiveness of the corrective actions.

Important notes about trend charts:

- It takes more than two points to establish a real trend. People often get this wrong simply due to hoping and wishful thinking. Two points can establish a line, but a second point in a time-data series cannot be differentiated from common cause variation. At least wait for the third data point and for the sake of accuracy, the more the better.

- Look carefully at trend charts to understand what the data is telling you. The chart below shows a downward trend over time. It also shows a point where the trend line crossed over the target line in a favorable direction. Context for any type of analysis, no matter how simple, is crucial for fully understanding the information.

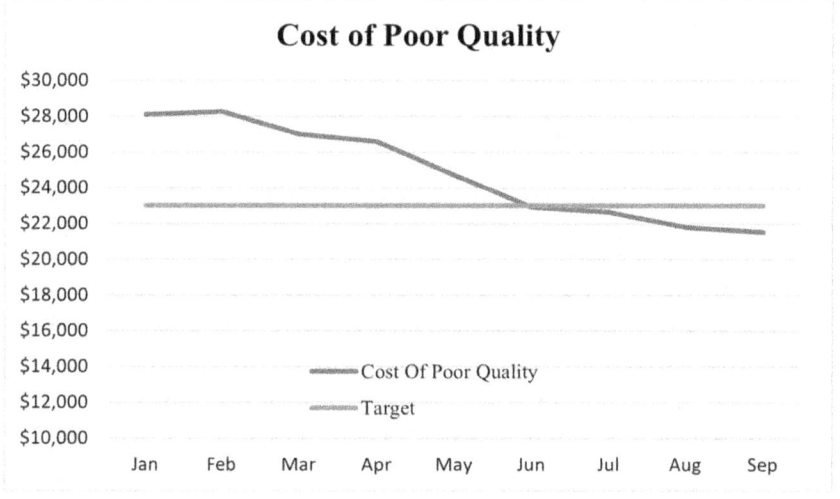

Figure 12.4 Trend Chart

List of Figures

I-1	Problem Solving vs Problem Fixing	10
1.1	8 Step Problem Solving Process Flow	17
1.2	Problem Solving Tools Selection Guide	19
1.3	Forrester Agricultural Products, Inc. Problem Case Study	20
2.1	Quality Alert	27
2.2	Containment Worksheet	29, 146
2.3	Containment Check Sheet	31, 145
2.4	Application Guidelines	32
2.5	Special Cause Variation Examples	35
2.6	Emergency Action Plan	39
2.7	Step 1 8-Step Report	41
3.1	RASIC Matrix for Problem Solving	45, 168
3.2	Step 2 8-Step Report	48
4.1	5W2H Matrix	52
4.2	Completed 5W2H Matrix	53, 136
4.3	Step 3 8-Step Report	56
5.1	Containment Action Plan	61
5.2	Step 4 8-Step Report	62
6.1	Root Cause Analogy	64
6.2	Problem Categories (Example)	67
6.3	FAPI Process Map	73, 167
6.4	Brainstorming List	76, 141
6.5	Cause & Effect Diagram – 1	78
6.6	Cause & Effect Diagram – 2	80, 144
6.7	Nominal Group Technique	82, 163
6.8	Pareto Diagram of Gear Damage	84, 164
6.9	3-Legged 5 Why Analysis	84
6.10	The Nail and the Kingdom	87
6.11	FAPI 5 Why Analysis – Why Made	89, 137

6.12	Example Good Linearity	92
6.13	Example Bad Linearity	93
6.14	FAPI 5 Why Analysis – Why Not Detected	98
6.15	Step 5 8 Step Report	100
6.1	Example PICK Chart	104
6.2	Completed PICK Chart for Corrective Action	105, 165
6.3	Permanent Corrective Action – Action Plan	106, 138
6.4	Pareto Chart – Post C/A (Validation)	107
6.5	Step 6 8-Step Report	109
8.1	Control Plan	114, 147
8.2	Updated FMEA	115, 151
8.3	Feed Across/Feed Forward Matrix	118, 150
8.4	Step 7 8-Step Report	120
9.1	Step 8 8-Step Report	124
10.1	Problem Solving Languages	129
11.1	Problem Solving Review Team Process Map	134
12.1	Capability Study	143
12.2	Layered Process Audit Process Map	158
12.3	Measles Chart	160
12.4	Trend Chart	169

Bibliography

Evans, Henry J. *Winning with Accountability: The Secret Language of High-Performing Organizations*. CornerStone Leadership Institute, Dallas. 2008. PP 8, 10.

Harper, Mercy. "What Are the Four Types of Benchmarking?" *APQC Blog*, APQC, 13 Nov. 2019, www.apqc.org/blog/what-are-four-types-benchmarkingAPQC Blog.

"International Standard ISO-9000:2015." 15 Sept. 2015.

Layered Process Audit Guideline. AIAG, 2014.

Lee, John L. *Rising Above It All: The Art and Science of Organizational Transformation*. iUniverse, 2012.

Liker, Jeffrey K. *The Toyota Way: 14 Management Principles from the World's Greatest Manufacturer*. McGraw Hill Education, New York. 2021. PP 258, 262.

"Process." *Merriam-Webster.com Dictionary*, Merriam-Webster, https://www.merriam-webster.com/dictionary/process. Accessed 21 Feb. 2021.

"Quality Glossary." *ASQ*, 20 Feb. 2021, asq.org/.

What Is Problem Solving? ASQ.org, 20 Feb. 2021, asq.org/quality-resources/problem-solving.

Yokoten. https://www.gembaacademy.com/resources/gemba-glossary/y Accessed 23 June 2021

www.ingramcontent.com/pod-product-compliance
Lightning Source LLC
Chambersburg PA
CBHW060837220526
45466CB00003B/1137